May we progress together, all
the way "to the unicorn."
Thanks and all my best,
        Dr. B. Bradell

READER COMMENTS

One advantage of writing a book online in weekly installments is that you get abundant feedback along the way. I have received thousands of pre-orders for the book, and with most of them, insightful comments, often documenting very impressive results. Here are a selected few, served up as "appetizers." Don't "eat" them all, but skim to the ones that resonate. Thanks,

— *Dr. Bridell*

What a contrast this diet is with some of the latest fad diets. I went by the diet shelves at the bookstore the other day and couldn't believe some of the junk that is there . . . It seems that Americans will buy (and try) any crazy diet anyone can come up with. But your diet, Dr. Bridell, is simple, stable, sensible and sustainable, and I thank you for it. R.E.

All of your concepts just ring TRUE. K.S.

After looking at and trying nearly every diet out there, your whole program has made total sense to both my husband and me. So far I have lost 20lbs. and he has lost 50, and we have not gained any back. Thank you very much for your timely and inspirational series. We're really looking forward to sharing the book with our children!! E.E.

Dear Dr. Bridell, I know you get lots of letters of gratitude for helping people lose weight. I want to thank you for something else. Thanks for teaching me how to enjoy food. Eating is now a delight, even though (or perhaps because) I eat only half as much as I used to. And guess what? You are right about food being a metaphor, because in learning how to enjoy eating, I have learned how to enjoy life! R.M.

––––––––––

A life-changing approach to weight loss. M.S.

––––––––––

I know this "diet" works! It's totally in harmony with the gospel. How can it not! J.H.

––––––––––

I have lost 70 pounds with the Bridell eat-half diet since last summer. It is the only diet I have ever tried that works and then just keeps on working. It is also the only diet that I have not absolutely hated after the first few weeks. B.B.

––––––––––

I have already enjoyed sharing the concepts and incorporating them. It has been a spiritual journey. V.H.

––––––––––

I found hope on both the physical and spiritual level. I must have this book. It has given me the only hope I have felt in years of dieting. FB

––––––––––

It is definitely more than a food issue for me. I like the spiritual approach to focus on life management. L.M

––––––––––

When I first started, "eat half" was a challenge. After all, if I was eating a dozen chocolate chip cookies a day, then would I lose weight if I only ate six? But when I stopped snacking, and truly cut down my portion sizes, the light bulb went on. I've lost 30 pounds. T.K.

I absolutely swear by the eat-half diet, and I loved the spiritual advice too. K.S.

———————

From the beginning, I have felt that this is the answer for me because I had come to the realization that my weight issue and my spiritual progress are tied together. M.M.

———————

The words and spirit of the whole diet resonates with me—with my soul. D.M.

———————

Your ideas are so different from the usual run-of-the-mill diet because you use gospel principles. I think this is the only way we can really achieve anything of value. J.G.

———————

Your diet has given me thoughtful reflection on a lot of habits or attitudes I did not even know I had . . . has made me more aware of choices in a lot of areas. K.P.

———————

As I read, your diet feels like revelation. P.W.

———————

I began reading it because I was interested in losing weight, but my motivation became much deeper as the weeks went by. D.C.

———————

It has been so refreshing to see a common sense and reasonable way to handle weight problems. I am grateful as one of those fed up with the usual "diet" fads and have appreciated your wonderful ideas. They have worked wonders in my life. C.W.

This has been a great journey for me. I have been amazed at the way I have been taught the gospel through this diet, which has addressed the spirit as well as the body. L.S.

———

Your diet is easy to follow and doesn't require special equipment, hassle, or frustration! R.S.

———

My husband lost 36 pounds in six weeks using your diet. Everyone wants to know how he has lost all this weight; we have [referred] many people to your diet. When he went to see his doctor he wanted to know how he was able to lose the weight. Now the doctor has given your web address to at least five of his patients! J.G.

———

We have decided to start an Enrichment health class using your chapters as text and adding exercise ideas and group support to help us all with the life changes essential to lose weight and reach optimum health. A.B.

———

It's the first diet that has been articulated to what I have always believed a diet should be. Yes, it works because it encompasses the total person and not just the physical side of dieting. B.N.

———

As a physician, I say thanks for your work and insight. I agree with your concepts and fundamental ideas. L.S.

(Testimonials continued in back of book)

Dr. Bridell's

LOGICAL AND RATIONAL

— & —

POETIC AND BEAUTIFUL

— & —

COMPLETELY GUARANTEED

EAT-HALF

DIET

(for <u>all</u> of your appetites)

BY THE MYSTERIOUS

DR. BRIDELL

Meridian Publishing
10504 Sideburn Court
Fairfax, VA 22032-2600
U.S.A.

Visit www.DrBridell.com
and write to DrBridell@meridianmagazine.com

Printed in the United States of America
ISBN: 978-1-934537-01-5
Cover and interior design by Scott Eggers, Salt Lake City

GUARANTEE TO ALL READERS/IMPLEMENTERS

1. You will lose weight–quite a lot of weight in most cases.

2. Your weight loss will actually be the least important thing this book does for you.

3. If 1 and 2 don't prove to be true, I'll give you your money back.

– Dr. Bridell

TABLE OF CONTENTS

Acknowledgments
Introduction: Candor, Appetites, Guarantees, Reasons and Results

First Intermission: The Other Appetites

Second Intermission: Giving Free Rein to Our Spirits

ACKNOWLEDGMENTS

Thanks to Meridian *and to Scot and Maurine Proctor for running the column and publishing the book. Thanks to Kathy Kidd and Darla Isackson for excellent editing. Thanks to Scott Eggers for art and design. And thanks to thousands of readers/dieters for your good input and good results.*

INTRODUCTION

Candor, Appetites, Guarantees, Reasons and Results

Completely candid honesty! That's one of the things that will set this diet apart from the rest. So let's start with this: "Dr. Bridell" is a pseudonym, and I'm not a doctor. I'm not a dietitian either or an exercise therapist or anything else that would give me even the remotest credential for writing a diet book. What I am is basically a practical person who is interested mostly in results. I'm also a writer who keeps noticing that diet books are always on the best-seller list. (And most of them promise far more than they can deliver and never address the emotional and spiritual causes of our physical problems.) What I like about the subject of dieting is that it's current, it's present, and it's about the now–about our daily habits and routines, about what you're going to eat today and tonight. You can start trying it right now.

I don't know a thing about calories or fat grams or metabolism or antioxidants or even proteins or carbohydrates. In a way this ignorance is bliss. I don't get confused about why the experts keep changing their minds about what is really good or bad for you. But I do know–absolutely–a couple of important things:

1. I know a way anyone can lose weight, for sure, for real, and keep it off and be healthier than ever before . . . and actually enjoy the process;

2. I know there is a direct, unbreakable connection between human happiness and the control of human appetites–and I don't just mean the appetite for food.

So, again, I have no credentials, nothing other than my absolute, outlandish claim that I know a simple diet that really works–for everyone! And that the same principles that make the diet work also apply to other appetites and thus make other things work better too—such as life!

Just how sure am I about this? Well, as you noticed on the first page of the book, I'm sure enough to guarantee it. You try this diet, and if it doesn't work, I give your money back—and you can keep the book, give it to someone else if you want, see if it works for them, and then maybe take it back and try it again. And remember, this isn't the publisher giving you this money-back guarantee, this is me, personally. Most authors only get fifteen percent tops, so if more than fifteen percent of you want your money back, I lose. So be it. It won't happen because this stuff works. That's not just a personal testimonial. This book was an online column before it became a book, and some of the testimonials that poured in are included in this book. Actually, the total weight loss, just of those column-readers who took the trouble to write in and tell me about it, was over two tons! I have made the world a lighter place!

There are lots of good reasons to go on a diet: to feel better, to think better, to work better, to play better, to look better, to live longer. The bottom line is that we really are what we eat, so there is genuine merit in having some kind of strategy for what we put into our mouths (and what we don't).

Who Should Read It

Who is this book for? Well, first, it's for folks who've tried other diets that didn't work, or didn't work for very long or who heard about other diets and knew, without even trying them, that they wouldn't work or that they couldn't stand them or couldn't do them. And, it's for people who want to go beyond food control toward gaining control of all appetites. This book is for people who want a higher, more intelligent, more spiritual approach—those who want to understand and then to win the greatest of all personal battles: the battle between one's spiritual entity and one's physical appetites.

There are way too many diet books out there, and most of them, in the long run, do more harm than good. (You may notice the continuing tone of candor here, and that candor may get so pronounced in future pages that you will understand why the mysterious Dr. Bridell does not wish to have his location or his true identity revealed.)

Anyway, there are lots of diet books available, lots of promises, lots of bunk. This one is different. It will present a series of concepts, starting with the deceptively simple, and building to a deeper understanding of what a diet really should be and why it should be thought of spiritually rather than physically.

Levels

Remember as you read (particularly the first few chapters) that all physical things are types or metaphors for the deeper reality of the spiritual. I think God could have devised any number of methods for refueling our physical machines. We could have plugged into trees or had some kind of built-in solar batteries, for instance. But he gave us the food method, with all of its nuances and variety and with the marvelous aspects of taste and appetite. Why? Because it is a way of learning about mastery and the relationship between body and spirit that apply to all aspects of life and eternity. Once learned, these lessons provide us with the tools we need to find and create the mortal joy we were sent here to experience.

If those concepts don't make sense to you yet, don't worry. I promise you that by the end of the book you will be able to go back and read the previous paragraph, and it will seem absolutely elementary–and absolutely true.

Maybe you've had a discussion something like the one I had on an airplane the other day sitting by a scientist I had just met who was telling me that man was just an advanced animal–perhaps not even the most advanced. (She really liked dolphins.) I must have looked disagreeable, because she challenged me to name a really substantive "difference in kind." She had already minimized the physical and mental differences as "differences in degree." Judging her to be unreceptive to spiritually-oriented ideas, I tried this one: Men and animals are polar opposites–180 degree opposites–in terms of their purpose and the manner in which they "fulfill the measure of their creation." (I used different words, of course, but you see what I was saying.) My punch line was this: "Animals become all they can be by following their instincts and appetites. Humans become all they can be by mastering and controlling their instincts and appetites."

Thus, I want you to think of this diet as an exercise or an experiment in fulfilling the measure of your creation. Food is just part of the laboratory or the gymnasium we call mortality. And the diet works on many levels, the first of which is the physical.

Final Introductory Thoughts

Two more thoughts for now, to prepare you for the rest of the book:

1. We already have the greatest diet ever devised, and it comes from our Heavenly Father, and it is called The Word of Wisdom. But we oversimplify it and overlook its nuances. One way to view this book is as an interpretation of The Word of Wisdom.

2. Remember: this book is really about joy and love. Alma told his son Shiblon to bridle all of his passions that he might be filled with love. (See Alma 32:12.) And the best definition I know of joy is winning the ongoing battle between spirit and flesh, between discipline (or discipleship) and appetites.

THE

PHYSICAL

DIET

THE BASIC CONCEPT OF
THE EAT-HALF DIET

There are so many good, natural, tasty, nourishing things on this earth to eat, and guess what? Your body wants all of some of them and some of most of them and needs some of most of them! Diets that eliminate all the carbs, or all the proteins, or even all the fats are taking away things your body needs.

At its best, your appetite, far from being your enemy, can be the sensor that tells you what your body needs. Your appetite probably isn't doing that for you right now because you've messed it up a bit. But you can fix it to where the things that sound the best to you–or look or smell or taste the best to you–actually are the best for you. Our appetites are good, our senses are good, the earth is good; and natural food, in all its variety is good.

The problem is that appetites don't know when to quit. They tell us what we want, but they don't tell us how much of it we need. There's no overload bell or back-up beeper.

So here's the deal: Eat what you want, but only eat half of it (half of your normal portion, half of what your appetite wants.)

Simple as that sounds, here's why it makes sense:

On average, Americans eat about twice as much as they need. One reason we are likely to eat more than we need is that the quality of the food we are eating is poor. It takes twice as much bad food to provide the essential nutrients we can get from half as much good food.

So what could be simpler? Eat what you want but only eat half of it, half of what you are accustomed to eating. Over time (a fairly short time actually) your body will adjust and start being more selective in what it tells you it wants, since it is getting only half as much. Vegetables and fruits will gradually look better; junk foods and "fluff" foods will start to look worse.

One rare and unique thing about this diet is that it's actually easiest to implement when you're eating out. At restaurants, you order what you want and they bring you, on average, twice too much–twice as much as you need. You eat half of it–half of each thing on the plate.

If your mother, in addition to telling you to clean your plate, told you that the children in India would starve if you didn't finish your food, then you may have a hard time throwing half of your meal away. So have it boxed or wrapped up and give it to a homeless guy on your way home, or to your teenager or your dog when you get home. As a last resort, eat it yourself–but for an upcoming meal, not for a midnight snack.

The principle is the same for eating in as for eating out. Just make half. (Be honest–you know what half is!) If you're not the "maker," just take half servings.

In theory, it's totally simple. Eat three "half-meals" a day. And you can also get away with a couple of half-snacks. But nothing else, nothing in between. What's hard is quitting when half is gone. It's hard to shut down–not to fudge. It's hard, but it gets easier. Your discipline increases even as your body (and stomach) adjusts.

That's it. That's the core and the essence of the first part of the physical diet. And that is your first implementation challenge. The next few chapters are essentially practical suggestions and methods to make it easier, more interesting, and more fun to "eat half," so don't be discouraged if this simple theory sounds difficult. More help is on the way!

WHAT YOUR BODY
WILL DO FOR YOU

With a concept as simple as the challenge in chapter one (just eating exactly what you already do, but cutting each food you eat in half and stopping when that first half is gone), you'd think there would now be some more complicated follow-up chapter that outlines just what you can and can't eat. You might expect me to tell you how to count fat grams or calories or carbs and instruct you to buy herbs or supplements or organic food. In other words, if chapter one is about the quantity (eating half) then chapter two must be about the quality, right?

Yes and no. Yes, this second chapter is about quality and nutrition, but no, it doesn't require you to count anything or plan elaborate menus or buy specific kinds of food. In fact, it isn't about you doing anything for your body. It's about what your body will do for you as a reward for the effort you make to eat half as much.

As your body gets used to less quantity, it will start demanding more quality. Vegetables and fruits and grains will become more appealing. As you continue to discipline your intake to half, you will essentially be training and developing a more selective appetite. Remember that you are not trying to kill or eliminate your appetite; rather, you're conditioning it so it will give you more joy and better results.

The secret to this whole diet is this: Your body knows what it needs. Every cell in your body knows what it requires to stay alive and to thrive. But your body doesn't wrest control from your appetites and obsessions and bad habits unless you train it to.

The body is an instinctive mechanism. Unlike the mind, which can choose and determine its own thoughts, the body–untrained and ungoverned–will take the path of least resistance. Thus, if you're eating twice as much as you need, and much of it is junk food or other unhealthy stuff, your body doesn't fight you, as long there's enough food coming in to provide what your cells need.

Say your body needs "3n" of nutrients each day, and it can extract that much from a "6v" volume of fairly bad food. Your body is okay with that even though much of the 6v may be making you fat or tired or full of cholesterol. If the food you're eating gets even worse in quality (say it now takes 8v volume to get the 3n of nutrients), your body will push you to eat even more.

But what happens if the mind takes control by "eating half" and limits the body to 3v volume of food per day? If it's all the same fairly bad food, the body will be getting only 1-1/2n and the appetite will push you to eat more. But if the mind stays strong and holds the quantity line at 3v, the only recourse your cells have is to work on the quality. Gradually, you start craving better, more nourishing, more wholesome food until your body can get its 3n of nutrients from a volume of 3v.

Consequently, if you stay true to phase one (eating half as much), your body will gradually give you the gift of phase two (craving quality instead of quantity). Your tastes (as well as your taste) will change, your body will lose weight, and every one of your cells will be happier.

Can it really be that simple? Absolutely! But simple things are often incredibly hard. How in the world are you going to eat only half as much food? If you've tried it for even a day or two, you know how hard it is! How can you do it–not for just a meal or a day or a week, but from now on? It is an extremely difficult proposition because any weakness in your conscious, choice-making mind will be exploited mercilessly by your instinctive body and your subconscious appetites.

And nobody else can do it for you. No one can make it easy or give you some magic pill. What I can do for you—what this book is written to do—is to motivate you by making the whole idea as appealing as possible by giving you some interesting and stimulating new ways to think, and by helping you see that not only the results will make you happy, but the process. Eating twice as slow and half as much, as you get used to it, is more enjoyable than the way you eat now.

The thing to work on first is the "slow" part. Make your bites smaller and chew them longer, so that eating half as much takes as long as eating twice as much used to. Think quality over quantity. Sip, smell and savor instead of guzzle, gulp and gorge. But wait, I'm getting ahead of myself. That is in the next chapter.

CHAPTER

SIP, SMELL, AND SAVOR

Let's start by thinking for a minute about how dogs eat. It's pretty ugly. It's like a race. It's like they're worried that something or someone will get their food before they can gulp it down. Their eyes dart around. They are protecting their food and trying to eat it before anyone else can get it or take it away. Taste, for most animals, seems to exist only in the form of salivating, instant gratification as they gorge, or maybe in the form of a warning that something they're trying to eat may be rancid or toxic. They bolt things down too fast to really taste them.

Unfortunately, our own eating patterns aren't as different from dogs as they should be. We often "snarf" our food, eating by instinct and appetite rather than by taste. Humans ought to eat in a completely opposite way from how dogs eat.

As we explored in Chapter 2, there is something starkly simple and perfectly proportionate about the Bridell diet. Eat half as fast (or twice as slow) and it will then take the same amount of time to eat half portions as it used to take to eat the whole thing. And as you get used to eating twice as slow and half as much, you will crave half as much and enjoy twice as much. (Isn't it nice how every one of those "halves" and

15

"twices" works in your favor?)

Most people say they enjoy eating, but hardly anyone makes a conscious effort to really appreciate and taste their food every time they eat. The three G's–guzzling, gulping, and gorging–seem to be much more common than the three S's–sipping, smelling, and savoring.

Eating can be and should be one of the best things in life, one of the simple pleasures. When it is thought of and pursued as a pleasure, it is done slowly and observantly and can involve all five senses. Good food's color and design and preparation can be appreciated by our eyes, its aroma by our noses, its texture by our touch, its remarkable taste by our tongues and different parts of our mouths. Even the through-the-bone sounds of food being thoughtfully chewed can be part of the sensual symphony.

As with anything else in life, the more we pay attention to the finer points of eating, the more pleasurable the consumption of food becomes, and the better we become at enjoying it. We also become more discerning, more discriminating, and thus more selective about what we eat.

When eating is routine or habitual or compulsory, we hardly taste or enjoy the food. We just stoke ourselves like throwing coal in a furnace; we fuel up like pumping gas into a car.

Sometimes, when we do taste and savor our food, it's only for the first bite or two. We enjoy that initial taste and then settle into the routine of eating. A little of this "diminishing return" is natural; the first run down the ski hill is always the most exhilarating. But we can train ourselves to enjoy the last bite of a meal almost as much as the first. Part of how we do this is taking only half as many bites; better yet, we can make every bite half as big.

Say that an "average" eater (guzzle, gulp, and gorge) eats a meal in twenty big, hurried bites. The first bite tastes good and every subsequent bite a little less good until most of the meal is just refueling or obeying the appetite. Now, say a skilled and artistic eater (sip, smell, and savor) eats half as much but takes the time to really enjoy each bite, perhaps splitting his ten bites into twenty smaller, more tasted and appreciated amounts. His enjoyment of each subsequent bite diminishes more slowly, and he ends up with twice the total pleasure though he ate only half the food. Let's say the numbers below represent the enjoyment factor of each bite. (The left column is the twenty bites of the guzzling, gulping gorger and the right column is the twenty divided or half-size bites of the smelling, sipping, savorer.) Remember that, since each bite on the right is half as big, the total food consumed in that column is half of the consumption on the left, yet the total enjoyment is twice as much.

Bite	Enjoyment	Bite	Enjoyment
1	10	1	10
2	8	2	10
3	7	3	9
4	6	4	9
5	5	5	9
6	4	6	8
7	4	7	8
8	4	8	8
9	4	9	7
10	4	10	7
11	3	11	7
12	3	12	6
13	3	13	6
14	2	14	6
15	2	15	5
16	2	16	5
17	1	17	5
18	1	18	5
19	1	19	5
20	1	20	5

Enjoyment Total:

75   **150**

Learn to take a little space between bites, like a lift ride between ski runs. Set your fork down between bites. Pause for a minute to reflect on the last bite and to anticipate the next. Like Edward Abby, who loved the desert because its stark simplicity allowed him to focus on the beauty of one single cactus plant, we need to separate and isolate each bite. Don't run your bites together into the rich profusion of gluttony. Space them like the sparse and appreciated single desert flower.

Paying attention, tasting, sipping, smelling, and savoring not only makes eating more enjoyable, it forces us to slow down. It replaces quantity with quality, decreasing the former and increasing the latter. Someone who focuses on the three S's will be more aware of the joy of good food. He will also notice things such as the slightly unpleasant, greasy feeling in the mouth or the processed, preservative aftertaste of food we should eat less of.

The tradeoffs of the "eat-half" approach are pretty good! You eat only half as much food but you double how long you chew and how much you savor. As quantity goes down, both the quality of the experience and (over time) the quality of the food goes up. You trade 50 percent of all the things that hurt (bulk, calories, fat, everything excess that's in there) for 100 percent more of all the things that help (enjoyment, time, discernment and superior nutrients).

Recognize, though, that a lot of American culture works against the quality-over-quantity, smaller-is-better mentality. Fast food chains encourage us to "super size" everything and people walk (or waddle) out of gas stations carrying 64-ounce jugs of soda. It's a little better in Europe where you might go to a British tea party and savor a tiny crumpet or stir afternoon tea with a miniature spoon before sipping it from a dainty cup. Or you might go to France and get a petite, six ounce soda can out of a vending machine.

The interesting thing is that smaller bites generate bigger flavor because there's room in your mouth to move the morsel around and to taste it with more parts of your tongue. It just feels better–not unlike a large spacious room with minimal fine furniture that seems more pleasant and tranquil than a cramped room stuffed with mediocre furnishings and knickknacks.

Along with eating less, you eat slower and better. There is a "second taste," a second wave of flavor that comes if we take smaller bites and chew and savor them a little longer. Almost as when a cow chews its cud, the well masticated morsels yield a smooth, blended aftertaste on each bite just before we send it off toward the appreciative stomach.

You begin to eat less like an animal and more like an artist. One aspect of this more artistic eating is the ability to focus on one bite of one food at a time rather than mixing things into a large artless mass in the mouth. Having a small amount in the mouth just works better, like a small load in a clothes washer; there's more space to tumble and taste the food.

Practice the art of eating half as much and twice as slow. As you do, you will begin to notice a higher level of awareness, and of enjoyment, and of discernment about what you eat. However, eating half as much will still be hard, and will still require discipline. I have some additional tips that can help, and one of the best and the simplest of them will be the subject of the next chapter.

MAKE WATER YOUR ALLY

One of the simplest ways to eat less food is to make less room for it by filling your stomach up with the beautiful, clearing, cleansing, lubricating, hydrating, zero-calories substance we call water.

Doctors and nutritionists have been telling us for decades that most of us need to drink more water–six to ten good sized glasses of it every day, they say. Not liquids–plain water. It's hard to drink that much unless we're sipping away pretty steadily.

One thing that can help us to hold our quantity of food intake to half is the habit of always drinking a big clear glass of water before you eat anything. Drinking a full glass before eating results in two good, simple results:

1. more water
2. less food

Both are accomplished by the simple resolution that becomes a habit: "Before I eat anything–meals or snacks–I will drink a full glass of water." Filling your stomach part way up with water is the simplest conceivable way to make less room in there for food. And staying fully hydrated (something very few of us do consistently) makes you feel better in all sorts of ways.

If you want to experiment a little and focus on how good water feels to your body, wait until a moment when you are quite thirsty, (after exercise perhaps, or first thing in the morning, or maybe when you get up in the night) and then drink a couple of glasses of cold water. Then lie down, relax, close your eyes and feel the hydration flowing through your body. If you concentrate you'll feel the water radiating out toward your extremities–refreshing, regenerating, replenishing, and renewing every cell.

More water really is the perfect complement to less food all day long. Get a good water bottle that you like the look and feel of, and carry it around with you. Have it with you in the car, set it on your desk, keep it near when you're watching T.V. or reading at home. Clean and fill it often. Let sipping become a habit.

It's the easiest thing in the world to monitor yourself to see that you are always fully hydrated. You'll be going to the bathroom more often, and your urine will be nice and clear. If you're not going several times a day and if your urine is yellow, you're not drinking enough.

Wow! Talk about a simple key to the eat-half diet! Just drink more! What a deal! It keeps you from eating more. It helps your body to digest better what you do eat, to use the nutrients more efficiently, and to get them distributed more effectively to your cells. It also helps your blood pressure, and (this is the amazing thing) it somehow makes you feel more relaxed, more calm, and even more optimistic. The best things in life are free, and one of the very best things is water!

One other thing water can do for you is to combat "impulse eating." Retailers thrive on impulse purchasing–shoppers who can't resist bargain-priced ticket items carefully placed where the eye glances and the hand can reach. Most of us eat in the same way impulse purchasers shop. When we walk past food, or notice food lying somewhere on the counter or in the drawer or on the shelf, we grab it and slap it into our mouths–just a little, of course, but it adds up. Some call it "grazing" because it's a lot like what horses do . . . just nibbling all the time. There's food all around us in our homes, so it can be a bite here and a bite there, not even counting the full-fledged snacks. We eat what's in front of us or around us for the same reason Sir Edmond Hillary said he climbed Everest: "Because it's there."

The problem with impulse eating is that it lets your appetite win—just in little pieces, but those small bites combine and multiply, and appetite wins while you lose (and gain). This has always been a tactic or a strategy in war and in sports . . . chipping away . . . a yard or two at a time . . . a foot in the door . . . slipping in under the radar. Little bites or nibbles can be so tiny they don't seem to matter. But that is the subtle, seductive strategy of appetite; it claims victory over us one little "innocent" bite at a time.

One way to bridle that appetite, to get rid of the grazing habit, is to sip water instead. Keep a water bottle close and replace the grazing habit with the sipping habit. Fill up on the water that helps you instead of the food that hurts you.

It's helpful to think of your appetite being like a horse. It wants to graze all the time. It's in the habit of putting its head down and nibbling. But you are the rider! You have the reins! You can pull that horse's head up every time he tries for a bite, and pretty soon you can break his grazing habit. Let him drink from the stream, but not eat from the field.

The only way to beat the grazing habit is to decide in advance to put nothing but water into your mouth between the meals and the one or two snacks you've chosen. Rein your appetite into complete submission on this. Show it who's boss. And let water be your ally!

CHAPTER

FIVE PER FORTNIGHT:
FINDING THE EXERCISE YOU LOVE

Putting less (and better) food into your body, and more water, is going to make your body work better. But you've still got to make your body work!

Should it be a chore, a task, a constant struggle to force this work to happen–to force your body to exercise? Does it have to be something you hate to do but keep pushing yourself to do anyway for your own good, like taking cod liver oil?

Exercising, like eating, should be one of the natural and simple and pure joys of life. It should feel good while you're doing it as well as when you're through, and it should be a way of rewarding yourself, not a way of punishing yourself.

The key is to find your form of exercise, to find the exercise you love, the one that makes your body smile while it's sweating out that pore-cleaning water and pumping those endorphins around through your expanded lungs and your healthier cardiovascular system.

For me, it's tennis. It used to be jogging, but now it's tennis–singles, without breaks between games, so that it's aerobic. For my spouse it's the bike–the road bike if the weather is good, or the stationery one at home if it's not. For my daughter, it's running; for my son, it's basketball. For my friend, it's the aerobic yoga class at a gym that has a good nursery for her two preschoolers. For another friend it's the stair master while he reads the morning paper every day. For another friend it's early morning half-court basketball.

For each of us, our chosen form of exercise can become a good habit. You can (and should) get so used to the habit of exercise that you don't even think about it. I would have to make a real effort not to play tennis. If I go for more than two or three days without a good match, I feel heavy, stressed, and nervous. If I'm traveling, staying somewhere without a court or an opponent, I have to run or bike or go to a gym (though I don't like it nearly as much) in order to satisfy my endorphin need.

I'm always looking forward to my next match and usually reflecting back happily on the last one (not so much if I lost). When I tore a knee ligament a couple of years ago and couldn't play (or run), I nearly went nuts until I found a trainer who convinced me that the injury was actually an opportunity to work on my upper body strength, which would make me a stronger and better player when my knee healed.

What I'm saying is that it is vital to find a physical passion of some kind–a form of exercise that you love. You don't need to instantly love it. It takes a little time to get into something, to get good enough at it that it's enjoyable, and to get psyched with the positive way it makes you feel. If you don't know what your physical passion might be, start trying things until you find one.

The point is that we all need an "output" to go with our improved "input." Disciplining ourselves with regard to our input into our bodies–less and better food and more water–has to be accompanied by the passion and rigor of the output of our exercise. One side is working on the quality and quantity of the calories we put in and the other side is developing the most enjoyable and beneficial way of burning and sweating them out!

Earlier generations didn't have to think or "strategize" nearly as much about the input or the output. Their hard physical work was the output, and it was usually so strenuous that it burned up all the input no matter what it was. But in our age of technology and desk or key-board jobs, we clearly need a well-thought-out and carefully-implemented strategy for both input and output. The point is that it can be an enjoyable strategy!

Depending on the type of exercise you choose, you may be able to do it every day, or it may be something you're only able to do two or three times a week (which is about the minimum frequency that will do much good).

Actually, the minimum ought to be five per fortnight. I like the British term "fortnight"–two weeks–because it gives more flexibility. Maybe you only get to your chosen exercise twice one week–so you crank it up to at least three the next week to meet the minimum of five per fortnight.

Find it! Do it! Love it!

CHAPTER

FASTING—AND SLOWING

For centuries, for millennia, forever, fasting has been associated with mental and spiritual clarity and with a cleansing and purging of the physical body. It can also help with the development of discipline that will make the "eat-half diet" really work.

As hard as it is to divide the food on your plate and eat only half of it, it is even harder (twice as hard?) to eat none of it at all. Periodic fasting re-calibrates your appetite, your sense of self-control, and even the size of your stomach.

In order to formulate my specific fasting challenge, let me define the terms and the timetable. For our purposes here, let's define fasting as going completely without food or drink for twenty-four hours essentially missing two meals and going from dinner on one day to dinner on the next day without eating anything in between. Make your fast day something you are disciplined about and determined to do.

Fasting once a month for twenty-four hours is not unique. Similar patterns are found around the world. For example, in addition to Mormons who practice it, Hindus often fast for the full day and night that accompanies each new moon.

Ten (mostly beneficial) results of a once-a-month fast are:
1. It clears out and rests your whole physical system.
2. It focuses your mind. You will think with new clarity about many things.
3. It enhances your "gratitude attitude" or your ability to feel and express thanks or appreciation (not just for food but for life at large).
4. It makes you more humble and more aware of your dependence on nature, on the earth, on God.
5. It fine-tunes your priorities and makes you more capable of separating the things that matter from the things that really don't.
6. (Being candid) It can make you feel nasty and short-tempered.
7. It can make you feel too weak to do anything.
8. It calms your mind and slows you down.
9. It gives you perspective as you think about and plan the month ahead.
10. It makes Dr. Bridell's eat-half diet seem easier. (After fasting, eating half seems like a luxury rather than a deprivation.)

Two negatives out of ten isn't bad, and numbers six and seven tend to fade as you get more used to fasting.

Let's focus on number eight for a minute–partly because I like the play on words, "fasting causes slowing." Think of some phrases we hear often these days (maybe say often): "If I could just slow time down a little," "There are not enough hours in the day," "So many tasks, so little time," "If I could clone myself maybe I could get everything done." Of these frequently-heard sentiments, one of them may actually be feasible–the first one. We will never have more hours, more time, or a second self, but it really is possible to slow time down a little.

When we get stressed and frantic and run around madly trying to get everything done, time seems to speed up just to frustrate us more. But sometimes, when we are calm and introspective, time seems to slow a bit and become more peaceful in its passing. One of the best ways I know to obtain a peaceful mind is to fast. During a fast one feels less nervous energy, less tendency to rush or to worry about detail. Fasting makes it easier to have perspective, to see the big picture, to focus in on what really matters. As this happens, time seems to slow down. Even a slightly clearer mind and slightly slower time are well worth the little bit of hunger you'll feel during a regular monthly fast. As a matter of fact, the hunger itself is a good thing, too. While you are fasting, hunger confirms that you are, at that moment, the master over your appetite for food. Your appetite says eat. You say no. Hunger confirms that you won.

A little hunger also enhances our sense of gratitude–and our empathy for the third of people in our world who feel hunger all day and who go to bed feeling it every night. And, if you are a person of spiritual inclination, fasting seems to be the perfect accompaniment to prayer, making spiritual contact with The Higher Power seem more direct and more natural.

CHAPTER

"REPAIR THE BREACH": GIVING
AWAY THE HALF YOU DON'T EAT

You may think your desire to lose weight is the only justification you need to live by the eat-half diet. However, there is a deeper and higher level of motivation that may also help.

Four thousand years ago, the prophet Isaiah foresaw our day. He predicted and warned about many things, none more graphic and haunting than his 58th chapter where he speaks of the growing gap or "breach" between the rich and the poor. (See Isaiah 58:12.)

Today we live in his prophecy. Each year the richest in our world get richer and the poor get poorer. The richest five percent of the planet's population control and possess more than fifty percent of the world's resources while the poorest thirty-three percent have only one percent of the world's wealth. This third of the world goes to bed hungry each night and sleeps on dirt floors.

As the breach gets wider, it destroys the happiness of both extremes. The poorest of the poor face insurmountable problems of hunger, thirst, disease, and lack of education. The richest of the rich (which, on a relative global scale, certainly includes a high percentage of Americans) face the opposite but potentially equally devastating (especially to kids) problems of boredom, indifference, instant gratification, and lack of appreciation or gratitude.

The gap or the breach is the enemy which undermines both sides. No wonder Isaiah challenged us to be, each in our own way, "repairers of the breach."

So what has any of this to do with the eat-half diet? Well, let's go back again to the "kids are starving in India" cliche so many of our mothers used to get us to clean our plates. While the cause and effect may not be as direct as Mom implied, children in Ethiopia and India are starving, and it is not completely beyond our capacity to help. Remember that no matter how wide the breach is, you become one of the "repairers" even if you close the gap one micro-sliver by feeding one hungry child.

In addition, making a small effort in that direction can have a positive psychological effect on our ability to observe and follow the eat-half diet. It completes the circle in a way. As we eat half, we give the other half to someone who benefits as much from having it as we benefit from giving it up.

Relatively easy ways to accomplish this include "sponsoring" a Third-World child for about $30.00 a month, or making small, regular donations to a local soup kitchen or homeless shelter. Doing something like this will complete the loop and add an interesting and beneficial form of motivation to your effort to consistently eat half.

Make your eat-less-and-give-more formula as mathematically accurate as you can. Even though you eat only half you will spend more than half as much money on the food you eat because as the quality of your food goes up, so will the cost. But make up a food budget for a week or a month while you are eating half. Then compare it with the estimate of what you spent before and find a way to give roughly the difference to those who are hungry.

Don't fall victim to the old "realistic" excuse about the problem being so big and global that you are obviously incapable of making a dent in it. Environmentalists don't recycle because they think they can rid the whole world of pollution; neither do they avoid aerosol cans because they think they can single-handedly fix the ozone hole. Instead, each one does what he does because it is his tiny part and because it is the right thing to do and because it makes him a stronger, better person. We can be like that—and like the beach walker who came upon a vast array of beached starfish and started throwing them back one at a time. An amused critic passed by and said, "There are too many. You'll never make a difference." The man threw another one out into deep water and said, "I made a difference to that one." He also made a difference to himself, to his character, and to his motivation—the same kind of difference you will make as you eat half and give half away.

Giving half to repair the breach in even the smallest way can give us empathy and help us see things as others see them. As we adopt some of the appreciation and awareness of those we help, our own lives become richer and our motivation to eat half grows stronger.

CHAPTER

POETRY: LIVING IN AND
SEEING THE MOMENT

Where are we going with this one? Poetry as part of a diet? Yes! And it's not as weird as you think. Here's the deal: This diet is all about awareness and sensitivity . . . Being aware of the quality and amount of what you eat . . . Appreciating it . . . Tasting it . . . Sipping and smelling and savoring. To improve and perfect our ability to do this, we have to work on improving and perfecting our ability to be aware and sensitive in the broader and more general sense. Awareness and sensitivity are qualities that can be developed, skills that can be learned and practiced.

There is no better way to do that than to attempt some poetry! (Have no fear, this is private poetry that no one will critique or judge. In fact, no one will even see it unless you happen to write one so good that you just have to show it to somebody.)

Think about the process of writing a poem; if you've never tried it, imagine what you think that process might be. First, you have to really notice something–become acutely aware of how it looks or sounds or feels or smells or tastes, and how it makes you feel. Second, you have to hold that image in your mind, to visualize it. Third, you have to discipline your-self to actually sit down and try to describe it, to write about it.

The awareness and visualization of poetry and the discipline of the eat-half diet are so similar. And the skills and perspectives you develop by trying to write poetry will help you become good at the diet.

Poetry can be about anything you notice and appreciate. Try to write some of your poems about your own body, about your appreciation for its form or some of its functions, about your visualization of how you want it to become, about the miraculous nature of its ability to assimilate high quality foods and turn them into energy and muscle.

Use visualization to heal and improve your body. Write poems about health and vigor. "See" yourself the way you want to be. Imagine, in vivid detail, your arteries carrying blood or your lungs assimilating oxygen or your antibodies warding off infection. Use poetry as a way of capturing these positive images.

The type of thinking required to support and enhance the eat-half diet is both analytic and artistic, part science and part creativity. Poetry (even bad attempts at poetry) provides the best way to mentally summon the combination!

Here's the challenge: Get a notebook or diary or some kind of little blank book that you can keep track of, and write something in it every day. It might just be one line of a poem, or a description of something you noticed that you can incorporate into a poem later. Some days you will be inspired and write a complete poem; other days you may just jot down a couple of lines, but the commitment to write something every day will cause you to be aware and to be looking and noticing more than usual.

Try thinking about where you are, what you can see or hear, what you are feeling, what your body is doing while you are eating. While you are sipping, smelling and savoring your half-portion of food, use the slowness of those moments to reflect a little, to let thoughts come into your mind, to try to be in the moment as you taste and appreciate your food. Open your book and write what you feel.

Poetry doesn't have to rhyme or follow some particular meter or structure. Just use the most graphic and clear words you can think of to describe what you are noticing or feeling. Use as few words as you can. Choose the words in the same way you are learning to choose your food, with quality being more important than quantity.

Here, as examples, are four poems written by implementers of my diet. None of them will win a prize, but writing them was helpful in noticing, helpful in slowing down, helpful in being in the present, and thus helpful in dieting. You can do just as well!

Liquid Light

The clear glass fills with clear water,
Bubbling up cold from tap to rim, catching light.
Then to my lips, a sip, a swallow,
    then a pulsing river flowing down,
Cooling and cleansing, pooling in the center of me,
Then trickling out through my tributaries to legs and arms
Some percolates back up, through another part of my neck
To cool and clear my brain.

Aerobics, First Day

A strange mood prompts me to see if I can survive an hour.
By happenstance I get in an advanced class.
The instructor is a girl shaped like a silver stovepipe,
Insufficient flesh to have curves and wearing shiny grey tights.
Even her hoarse voice is metallic, and she is bionic.
I realize it as she never stops, never tires or frowns or moans,
Never even sweats.
I do all of those things.
Each provides a modicum of relief.
The music pulses loud against the glitter and glass.
It's a disco really; strobe lights would look right in place,
Glistening bodies and leg warmers.
A new phenomenon combining narcissism and vanity
But a more obtainable pride than most
And not all bad (But don't ask my body!)

A Sky Like That

Leaving the office one routine day
glanced up and beheld
the glory bursts of heaven's sun
behind the gray receding storm clouds.
Late March after a day-long snow
now, air winter crisp, clarion clear.
Sky's pure, pale delicate blue
(since it's so new) and the still gray retreating clouds
with edges dazzling white,
giving away the presence of the sun.
They still try to hide –
Had I been all day in a great museum
unseen–studying works of master man
my reaction would have been the same
walking out: "This is beauty"
and all works of man fail to compare.

Early Light

Looked out this morning early light
long before usual
white round snow, white round moon, blue sky,
    gold only along east rim
even light, with no dominating source
part moon, part dawn, part snow-earth reflection
stereophonic light–or triphonic–or multi-phonic
comes from everywhere
bathes all the air with just enough illumination to see
and be moved by its beauty.

So try your hand at a poem or two–it is part of the eat-half diet!
And you can do it!

THE HORSE AND THE BRIDLE

Horse riders and horse lovers (I'm both) know how strong these magnificent animals are. They outweigh us by a factor of five or six to one, but that's just the beginning. Their tendon and muscle connections give them a leverage that probably doubles their weight advantage. I've been literally thrown across the barn by a horse that just got startled and lifted his head.

Because of their strength and their beauty, horses have been used by man for countless things, ranging from toil to pleasure. They have also been used since antiquity for one of the most apt metaphors in history.

"We put bits in the horses' mouths," said James, an apostle of the New Testament, "that they may obey us, and we turn about their whole body (James 3:3). To become "perfect men," he said, we must be "able also to bridle the whole body" which can include our expressions and our appetites (see James 3:2). And Alma made the beautiful and provocative statement, "See that ye bridle all your passions, that ye may be filled with love" (Alma 38:12).

One reason the horse is such a perfect metaphor is that horses are extraordinary, remarkable and beautiful creatures than can serve us in ways that are exciting and thrilling as well as useful. There is nothing quite like a horse at full gallop, especially if you are on its back, moving with it and feeling its grace and power.

If you focus only on the danger of a horse, only on its strength and potential to hurt you, you could begin to see the horse as an enemy, something you need to fight and subdue. One way to be sure a horse does not hurt you would be to tranquilize it or drug it to neutralize its strength. And a way to absolutely guarantee that a horse will not hurt you would be to kill it. But what a foolish and cowardly approach that would be, and how it would deny the beauty and the usefulness of the horse.

So it is with our passions and our appetites. These are not things we should want to kill or to medicate out of our lives. They are not our enemies, but our energies. They can be our motivators rather than our masters, and a thrill to ride rather than a threat to ruin.

But only with the bridle! Until we put the bit of our own control between the teeth of our urges and instincts, these appetites can injure us, wound our destiny, and throw us off the path of our dreams and our goals.

The last thing we should want to do with our appetite for food, or for sex, or for any of God's gifts is to dull it, subdue it, tie it up or hobble it so it loses its beauty and strength and passion–or to kill it. (Vows of celibacy seem a tragedy to me.) Rather, we should bridle our appetite, harness it, control it to work with us and for us instead of on us and against us.

Your brain is the bridle, and your mental commitment to eat half as much and twice as slow is the bit that can gradually come to feel natural and accepted in the mouth!

As you eat half, eat twice as slow and with twice the appreciation and enjoyment, keep the horse in mind; think of your soul as the rider and your will as the bridle. If it helps, try to visualize me, Dr. Bridell, (however you imagine me) handing you the bridle, helping you slip it over the horse's head, helping you to get the bit between its teeth, putting the reins in your hand, telling you to show the horse who is boss, to stay in control, and to enjoy the ride.

REVIEW OF THE PRINCIPLES AND PRACTICES OF THE PYSICAL DIET

In this tenth chapter, let's take a look back and review what we have covered so far in the Physical part of the diet. It is important to have the principles and practices well in mind both to implement the eat-half diet and to help comprehend the Mental and Spiritual parts of the diet which are still to come.

Simple Principles of the Physical Diet:
1. Natural foods, in all their variety, are good for the body.
2. Appetite, while it can direct us to the food our body needs, doesn't know when to quit.
3. We normally eat about twice as much as we need.
4. By eating half of that—half as much as usual (and holding the line and doing it consistently)—we will gradually gravitate toward food that is twice as good. (Our body, denied quantity, will demand quality.)
5. By eating half as fast we can enjoy food twice as much.
6. The more sensual attention we pay to eating, the more pleasurable it becomes.

7. Disciplining both the amount we eat and the pace at which we eat further enhances the pleasure.
8. Our bodies need more water as much as they need less food.
9. A stomach that is full of water will ask for and be satisfied with less food.
10. Fasting to let the whole digestive system shut down and rest periodically can cleanse and rejuvenate and re-calibrate capacity.
11. Mental and spiritual awareness are heightened and sharpened by fasting.
12. Regulating the "output" of exercise is as important as regulating the "input" of eating.
13. With some effort and attention, each person can find a form of physical exercise he or she loves.
14. Exercise, because of the endorphins it produces, can become a pleasurable positive habit.
15. Giving away the half we do not eat increases our motivation even as it feeds our brothers and pleases our Father.
16. Poetry or other artistic outlets enhance awareness, slow us down, orient us to quality, and increase our discipline.
17. The horse and bridle metaphor can help us visualize and implement the diet.

Simple Practices of the Physical Diet:
1. Eat half of your normal three meals a day and one or two half snacks. Nothing else.
2. Eat slowly. Sip, smell, and savor, so that eating the half takes as long as eating the whole used to.
3. Drink a tall glass of water before each half meal or half snack.
4. Fast for twenty-four hours once a month.
5. Exercise aerobically (find a form you love) for at least 30 minutes at least five times each fortnight.
6. Give the equivalent of the half you don't eat to those in need.
7. Write one or more poems per week. (Write something from your awareness every day.)

Do you believe these 17 principles? Can you implement these seven practices? Let your belief in the principles increase your motivation to implement the practices. Work at it! Don't give up! The results will be there if they are not already. And the results you see on your scales will be just the beginning.

FIRST INTERMISSION

THE OTHER APPETITES

Most good performances have an intermission, sometimes two of them—a time to get up, move around, ponder the first act and get ready for the next one. This is a good breaking point because, starting in the next chapter, we will begin to explore how the appetite for food is a "type" of all the other appetites that come with mortality. We will also see how the eat-half diet is a type for how we can control all of the other appetites.

As you have noticed, I was determined to stay with the "diet book" mentality for the first section of this book. However, you could probably tell that my tongue was partly in my cheek. What I really want to do is set up a model or a metaphor to talk about all appetites in general—which is my real interest and the real subject of this book.

That is not to say there was anything disingenuous or misleading about the physical food diet I've proposed to you. It does work. It will work for anyone who implements it. Not only that, its results will make you more capable of understanding and implementing the mental diet and the spiritual diet that follow.

The physical, mental and spiritual are not only connected, they are three parts of the same whole, and that whole is the soul. A physical body that is lean and clean, that is trim, strong, tuned and hydrated is infinitely better at receiving, conducting and supporting the mental and spiritual processes that happen within. And that re-tuning can open up the whole universe to us.

We need to be sure we don't shortchange the reasons for and the ramifications of the physical diet, reducing our motives down to things such as a more attractive appearance or smaller dress size. Instead, let's elevate the idea of the physical diet to purposes such as longer life, clearer insights, and a more pure intelligence and spirituality.

You have now read through the physical diet and decided (or are deciding whether or not) to do it. During this brief intermission, while you're thinking about it, let me add some other points (in the form of thought-prompting questions and observations) for you to ponder. I've mentioned some of them briefly before, but these points will lead us into the mental and spiritual diets I have in mind, and will begin to reveal where I'm really trying to take you in this book:

1. What if the God who made us could have used any means He wanted for us to "refuel" or to get the nutrients into our physical machines to keep them going (and growing)? He could have designed it so we just tapped a tree or a pond or some nutrient source through a tube or in some other utilitarian way, like gassing up a car. But instead, He made eating and drinking a pleasurable and infinitely varied experience and gave us appetites and tastes and expandable capacities. Why? Could it be that our food appetites are intentionally the physical representation of all our other appetites, and that by learning to control that most obvious appetite we can learn the principles that control all other appetites?

2. Perhaps the most stunning way in which man is different from animals is that animals reach their destiny and fulfill their purpose by following and being subject to their instincts and appetites while humans reach their fullest potential and gain their highest destiny by controlling and mastering their appetites. Perhaps our human qualities of patience and discipline, of the capacity to delay gratification and be proactive rather than reactive with regard to our appetites are the qual-

ities that separate us most dramatically from the animals.

3. The word "appetite" often carries a negative connotation unless it is modified by a positive adjective like "healthy." By itself it sounds a little like a foe or an enemy or at least an unpleasant challenge. In fact, appetites are what make life exciting. They are our passions, the very drives and urges that motivate us and that make life enjoyable. Yes, they require controlling, but even that can be a pleasure. Try to imagine a life without appetites and we find ourselves contemplating a flat, effortless, and boring state.

4. Could joy be defined as appetite control? Is self-mastery ultimately the source, or at least the trigger, of our happiness?

5. There may be not only a connection, but a wonderful sequence between body, mind, and spirit. These three may provide related but separate and appropriately sequential ways of knowing and understanding things, with the sensory method leading to the scientific method and finally being eclipsed by the spiritual method.

6. In this larger perspective, appetites may be perceived as the passions and potential joys that come with this mortal opportunity, and diet may be viewed as how we choose to think and to live while we are here on earth.

Expanding Our View of Appetites

So what are our other appetites? Think for a minute before you turn the page and read on. Think about what you would put on the list.

Without trying to be expansive or to sequence or categorize them in any particular way, here are some appetites:

Recognition	Position	Sex
Ambition	Sleep	Power
Ownership	Wealth	Control
Love	Independence	Understanding
Comfort	Knowledge	Fame (or visibility or credit)
Television and Media	Acceptance	Internet and Technology
Achievement	Games and Diversions	

With the list in front of us (and it could be much longer) let's ask some key questions: What are appetites? Are they things we need? Things we want? Things we desire? Are they instincts? Natural attractions? Something learned or something inherent?

With animals, appetites or instincts are built-in energy-and-purpose-producing urges that allow them to survive. Are they more or less than that with us? Are we best served by subduing them or celebrating them? Can we do both?

Are there good and bad appetites? Are our longings for things such as love or wisdom too high and too pure to be called appetites? Are those with stronger or weaker appetites higher or lower beings?

Do any of these questions matter?

Bridell's diet takes the view that they do matter–that they matter very much. Further, it takes the view that all appetites can be appreciated and understood and controlled by the same principles that work with our appetite for food.

The result of the physical diet is a body that is fit and strong and joyful. The result of the mental diet is a mind with the same characteristics. After a few more chapters devoted to the mental diet, we'll need another intermission to set the stage for the spiritual diet.

The physical diet and the loss of physical weight and the control of the appetite to eat is only the tip of the iceberg; the real challenge of mortality is to master and control all of our appetites. The appetite for food is a "type" for all other appetites, instincts, cravings, and desires. The principles that work for the physical also work for the emotional/mental and the spiritual constructs of life.

As you read on, compare the Physical chapters you have already read with the upcoming Mental chapters and note that they take the same sequence and apply the same principles. Go back, periodically as you read, to the corresponding physical topic, and use it as a "type" to better understand the Mental/emotional chapters you are currently reading.

The appetite for food and the physical Bridell diet will serve as the metaphor and the type for the mental and emotional self-discipline and appetite control we will move into in the coming chapters.

KEEP WORKING ON AND BEING COMMITTED TO THE PHYSICAL DIET!

Work on it and try to get better and better at it because it is not only to help you lose weight and become physically stronger. It will also be the key by which you understand the deeper elements of fulfilling the measure of your creation by mastering and controlling the instincts and inclinations of your body, mind, and spirit (your whole soul!).

THE
MENTAL
DIET

CHAPTER

"EAT-HALF" MENTALLY

I was climbing in the desert of Southern Utah when I wrote this chapter, (that is not, in any way, to be taken as an identity clue, because I do not live anywhere near Southern Utah). I found myself at the mouth of a mysterious cave on the face of a red cliff. The cave was beautiful, with three huge white calla lilies blooming at its mouth and a high chimney at the back that revealed the bright blue sky through the opening far above. A cooing dove lived somewhere up in that rock chimney (you should have heard the echo of her call). She flew straight down to check on me every once in a while and then flew straight up again to her nest. I found the place so appealing that I sat, cross legged and guru-like, on a rock shelf at the opening of the cave and began to write. (A couple of other hikers even stopped later on to ask me the meaning of life–and I referred them to this book.)

The desert is a lot like the eat-half diet. It is sparse. It is beautiful, but not in an overly abundant and gluttonous way. At the time of year I was there, it was in bloom, with yellow flowers on the cactus, and small, isolated blooms here and there in the sand. Because they are few and spread out, you notice each blossom, each cactus, each individual flower separately, appreciating its individual beauty, much like you enjoy food when you eat it one small, slow bite at a time. There is no junk here in the desert, no excess of vegetation, no stuff competing with other stuff.

What power there is in simplification, in getting rid of excess, in focusing on one fine and worthwhile thing at a time! What a good mental diet it is to consume about half–to avoid all the excess that life puts in front of you, to keep your focus on the relatively few things that really matter, and to try to get rid of all the stuff that doesn't.

A woman I know was going nuts with the busyness and stress of her life. Her three boys had endless lessons or games or practices after school, sometimes two or three a night. She finally sat them down and said "Boys, this is just too much. We never eat together, we have no time to just relax and talk; something has to go. I have decided we will not do soccer next year." Instead of the cries of disappointment she had expected, the oldest boy smiled sheepishly and said "Good, Mommy, because we really don't like soccer."

How many things in life are we doing just because everyone else is, or because we think we should, or because we want to keep up with the Joneses? Why do we let our lives become so overwhelming and so busy that we drive ourselves crazy doing things that may not really matter? e.e.cummings said something like, "More, more, more; what are we trying to become, morticians?"

The mental eat-half diet is about simplifying and cutting out the excess busyness of our lives. It is about losing the "weight" of stress and fatigue.

A good way to start is by writing a personal mission statement that defines what is really important to you, then cut out of your life the things that have nothing to do with your mission.

Another good way is to make a list of stewardship priorities each day:

- One special, need-based thing you will do for someone in your family
- One thing you will do for your church calling
- One meaningful, need-based thing you will do for yourself

These are the things that matter, and this is the mental diet that will help you lose the "pounds" of life's trivia and busyness that you don't want.

Watch less T.V. You don't need to turn it off all together, but pick one or two shows that you really love, and limit yourself to them. Go for a walk or read a book or have a good conversation with someone you love during the other two hours you might have watched.

Allow yourself a little solitude each day. Take a longer shower if that is the only place you are alone with your thoughts. Or go out in the garden and get your hands in the dirt.

Like the eat-half food diet (which is a "type" for controlling all other appetites), the mental diet is not about trying to "eat" or juggle more things, but about enjoying and taking time for the things that are truly good and that really matter. It's about grabbing hold of your life and making thoughtful decisions about what you do and about not just "eating" whatever is placed in front of you.

CHAPTER

WHAT LIVING LIFE AT
HALF-SPEED WILL DO FOR YOU

"The laws that govern our food intake can be extended to other areas of our lives. In many instances, our spiritual lives can be mirrored in our physical situations. Laws that govern the physical can also govern the mental.

The promise of the Physical diet (chapter 2) is that as you cut the quantity intake of food by half, your body will start desiring and demanding better quality in what you do put in your mouth. If you seek out quality nutrients, junk and fast food will look less appetizing, and vegetables and fruit will look better and better.

The same principle works with your mind. As you simplify–cutting some of the trash and non-nourishing stuff out of your life, your soul will gradually begin to appreciate and even crave more quality in your activities, your entertainment, your interests, and your relationships.

In the Physical diet, the key to eating half as much is to eat twice as slow. Slow down the way you eat–smaller bites, more chewing, savoring each morsel. When you do this your body rewards you by enjoying food more, craving quality, and getting fitter and stronger. In life we need to do the same thing. As you slow down and simplify the way you live and the way you think, your brain rewards you by producing better ideas and purer thoughts, by noticing more beauty, becoming more perceptive and more aware.

In our world today, the pace of life has become so fast. We rush from one thing to the next without taking time to notice or even to think. Some of us remember slower times when evenings were long enough to sit and talk and even have dinner together. Kids had time to just play and create, weekends were a time to relax and recharge, and summer had some lazy, hazy days.

Today, the average meal at McDonald's takes six minutes to consume, our evenings are busier than our days, our kids are as over-scheduled as we are, and we have developed what Guy Claxton, a British psychologist calls "an ever increasing inner psychology of speed, of saving time and maximizing efficiency, which is getting stronger by the day."[1] Everything seems to be geared to getting more done in less time.

Carl Honore, in his book *In Praise of Slowness,* puts much of our lives in perspective when he honors speed but also worries about it. He admits that we wouldn't want to live without jet travel or the Internet. However, the main thrust of his book is that our obsession with doing more and more in less and less time has gone too far.

He says, "Even when speed starts to backfire, we invoke the go-faster gospel . . . yet some things cannot, should not, be sped up. They take time, they need slowness. When you accelerate things that should not be accelerated, when you forget how to slow down, there is a price to pay."[2]

One London-based life coach indicates that burnout, which used to be something mainly found in people over forty is now common in the thirties, and even the twenties. Perhaps we would do well to remember what Mahatma Gandhi said: "There is more to life than increasing its speed."

Even our kids, who used to have both time and spontaneity, are now over-programmed. I'll paraphrase a recent cartoon that said it all: Two little girls are waiting for the school bus, each clutching a personal planner. One says to the other, "OK, I can't miss ballet, but I can leave gymnastics early, and cancel piano. If your Mom will move your violin lesson to Thursday and let you skip soccer practice, then we'll have an hour on Thursday the 20th to play."

Author Carl Honore said, "Not long ago, the New Yorker published a cartoon . . . two primary-school boys are walking down a street, books under their arms, baseball caps on their heads. With a world weariness beyond his years, one mutters to the other: 'So many toys–so little unstructured time.'"[3]

The culture of hurry gets even more intense for college students. The stress of trying to do everything and do it all fast got so intense at Harvard that the Dean of the Undergraduate school, Harry Lewis, wrote an open letter that now goes out to every first-year Harvard student. The title of the letter is "Slow Down."

During the course of seven pages, Lewis makes the case for getting more out of university–and life–by doing less. He urges students to think twice about racing through their degrees and to avoid piling on too many extracurricular activities. Do fewer things and take the time to make the most of them, he says, and remember that doing nothing at times, and slowing yourself down is an essential part of good thinking.

"Empty time is not a vacuum to be filled," writes the Dean. "It is the thing that enables the other things on your mind to be creatively rearranged, like the empty square in the 4X4 puzzle that makes it possible to move the other fifteen pieces around."

One lesson of the New Testament story of Mary and Martha may never have been more relevant than it is now. We find ourselves like Jesus described Martha–"cumbered about with much serving" and "careful and troubled about many things" (see Luke 10:40-41), trying to do everything for everyone and missing what really matters. We find ourselves unable to, like Mary "choose that good part which shall not be taken away from her" (Luke 10:42).

We need to consciously slow down. Slowing down physically can help us slow down mentally. Make yourself walk a little slower and notice a little more, drive a little slower and be more aware of what is around you. You will only lose a few seconds, and you will start to win the battle against haste and hurry. The old saying "haste makes waste" is true. Hurrying all the time not only makes us botch things, it wastes our peace and wrests the quality from our lives. How many times a day do we say "hurry" to our kids (or to ourselves)?

Find the things that calm you, that slow your mind down. For some it is gardening. For one man I know, it is archery–the solitude of shooting arrows at a target. For many, classical music is a soother and a slower of their souls.

We said earlier that everything seems to be geared to getting more done in less time. Well, think for a minute about all of your various appetites as interlocking gears, some bigger, some smaller, that turn together. Appetites for food, for success, for recognition, for wealth, for sex, for control, for status–all are gears turning.

What is the "drive gear," the one that powers all the others? Perhaps it is the appetite for hurry, for haste, for speed. We want everything faster. We overload our lives and think the way to get everything done is to hurry more. That sense of pace feeds each of our appetites and lets all of them pull harder on us.

If we can slow down one of those interlocking gears, that one begins to slow them all down and to resist the drive gear of hurry and haste. Our hunger for food, the appetite that serves as such a good metaphor for all the others, is a good place to start. By sipping and savoring small bites and eating half, we change the unhealthy rush of quick-quantity refueling to a pleasurable tasting of quality. And the very process of slowing down that gear begins to slow down the others. We taste, and while we are tasting, we start seeing more and hearing more, and thinking more.

If you can slow down eating, you start to feel that you can slow down other things. Let that kiss for your loved one take a little longer. Look into a person's eyes and hold the hand a second longer when you greet someone. Sit down and take a look around you for a moment before you start a piece of work.

Fast thinking, the kind of thinking we do under pressure (when the clock is ticking), often produces tunnel vision and reduces our awareness of the things around us. Slow thinking is intuitive and creative.

Slowing down and giving ideas time to simmer at their own pace yields rich and subtle insights. It leads to lateral thinking and serendipity.

The scriptures tell us to "be still and know . . . " (Psalm 46:10). I agree with Plato, who believed the highest form of leisure was to be still and receptive to the world. Franz Kafka put it this way, "You don't even need to leave your room. Remain sitting at your table and listen. Don't even listen, simply wait. Don't even wait, be quite still and solitary. The world will freely offer itself to you to be unmasked."[4]

As the mind slows down, one begins to discover something hard to explain logically, but wonderful to feel. It is "the speed of going slow." It is the seeming incongruity that as you slow down and become more peaceful and aware, you actually get where you are going or finish what you need to more easily and somehow more quickly. The lights turn green for you, the people you need answer their phone, and life takes on a more pleasant rhythm. Rudyard Kipling wrote of keeping your head while all about you are losing theirs. Today, we need to learn to keep our cool while all around us are losing theirs, and to stay slow inside even as we work to meet a deadline or to get the children to school on time.

The speed of going slow is not something one learns overnight, or that works all the time. But it is something one can learn and something one can practice. Eat slowly, walk slowly, think slowly, try for more awareness and perspective, taste more, see more, feel more, and look for more quality and less quantity in your activities, your relationships, and your goals as well as in your food.

CHAPTER

SIPPING, SMELLING AND
SAVORING YOUR LIFE

When our food appetite controls us, we rush through meals, gorging ourselves, animal-like, and missing much of the taste and enjoyment. When our other appetites, lusts, and instincts control us (particularly the pervasive appetite for hurry and haste), we rush through our days, missing much of the beauty and subtlety that makes life worth living.

On the other hand, when we control our food appetite, sipping, smelling, and savoring our food rather than gorging, gulping, and guzzling it, we can appreciate and taste every morsel. When we control our other appetites (for work, for control, for instant gratification, and especially for haste) we begin to find the moments of joy that are the very purpose of life.

We have focused on doing things slower to gain more awareness. Now think about it in reverse. Can being more aware enable us to slow down?

Stress-producing haste and impatience often comes from a habitual focus on the future. We are thinking about where we need to be and what we need to do, and with our mind out there in front, we pull ourselves headlong through the present, not even noticing the beauty, the people and the opportunities slipping past us.

Telling (and willing) ourselves to slow down (Chapter 12) is important, but the other half of the formula is to increase our observational powers and our awareness of what is around us–of living more in the present and appreciating the moment we are in. Those who learn to do this receive many rewards:

1. Enjoyment of both the sensual and the spiritual beauty that is always around us

2. Serendipitous acquaintances, opportunities, ideas, and even short-cuts to where we are trying to go

3. A slower, less stressed attitude that makes us somehow more efficient (the speed of going slow)

Of course we need to think ahead, to plan, to make our lists. But once they are made, we need to learn to shift back into the present and notice and enjoy all that is here. After all, the present is the only place we ever actually live!

Some people can induce an inner calm just by commanding themselves to slow down (eating slower, walking slower, etc,). Others, like a horse straining at the bit, just become more jumpy and anxious when forced to go slower.

The key for this second type of person is to focus on awareness instead of on slowing down. Do what you need to do: Run your errands, check off your list, make your calls, feed the family, get the kids ready, do your work–but while you are doing it, tune in to the present that is all around you. Be aware of smells and sounds. Notice and appreciate things as well as just seeing them. Feel textures, and really taste what you eat. In other words, sip, smell, and savor your life rather than gorging, gulping and guzzling it.

The reason the eat-half food diet works is that as we eat less and eat slower (reducing quantity), we enjoy more (increase quality) and are motivated to continue the pattern. As we become better and better at enjoying more–at sipping and savoring–we find it easier and easier to eat slower, and to eat less.

It is a classic chicken and egg situation. Whether you start with the "egg" of slowing down or with the "chicken" of enjoying more, one will lead to the other, and you will have both. With all appetites, slowing down increases awareness and enjoyment, and increasing awareness and enjoyment causes a slowing down.

With eating, the first bite or two is easy to enjoy because you are hungry and the food tastes good. But as you shovel the rest of the meal in, satisfyinging the appetite, the joy per bite quotient drops. It takes awareness and conscious decisions to sip and savor to keep the enjoyment level up.

"First bites" in life are also easy to enjoy—the first time in a new place, the first ski run of the morning after a snowstorm, the first day of school or a new job or a new relationship. But when routine and the pressure to get everything done sets in, we find ourselves just getting through the day rather than enjoying it. We rush around without awareness, satisfying our appetite to get things done, but not enjoying much of it along the way. By conscious awareness, we begin to notice things that bring back the joy.

Our senses are intended to be the receptors of joy. The better we use them and tune them, the more we receive. I once met a blind man in the busy center of a city, sitting quietly on a street corner with his dog, selling baskets he had made. As I spoke with him, he must have detected pity in my tone, and he didn't like it. Politely but firmly he told me that while I had one sense (sight) that was better than his, he had four that were better than mine. He then proceeded to tell me of sounds and smells he could sense that I could not, and things he could feel and taste, even in the clamor of the city. He even told me some things about myself that I don't know to this day how he perceived. His joy came from his awareness, not from rushing around doing things.

Learn to sip and savor your life, to appreciate new perspectives, to relish the beauty and intrigue of the present, to fine tune your senses, to live in the moment. See your senses and your awareness as an antidote to your appetites. Let them slow you down and bring you peace.

THE CLEAR WATER OF
THOUGHT AS YOUR ALLY

As I sit down to write this morning, I have my favorite water bottle sitting on the table beside my keyboard. I will sip away at it, and by the time I finish this chapter I will likely have finished the one liter it holds, and be halfway to my daily goal of drinking two liters of water. Full hydration is a big part of the Bridell diet. This pure, clear H2O is what cleanses and lubricates and refreshes the body. I take this favorite bottle pretty much wherever I go. It's in the cup holder when I am driving and on my desk when I'm at work. If I'm a little behind on my water consumption, I even take it into the shower with me. It makes the two liter a day goal easy.

Earlier, we advocated making water your ally in the Bridell diet by getting in the habit of drinking a full glass of water before each meal. A stomach full of water doesn't have room for too much food. Chapter 4 said that drinking a full glass of water before eating results in two good things: more of the water your body needs and less of the food it doesn't need.

Filling your stomach part way up with water is the simplest conceivable way to make less room in there for food. And staying fully hydrated makes you feel better in all sorts of ways.

The same principle and habit works in the mental diet, but the clear water is replaced by clear thought, and the habit we need to develop is to always drink in some pure thought before we shift into eating away at any kind of action.

Scripture tells us that God created all things spiritually before He made them physically (see Moses 3:5). What a lesson. Think things through before trying to do them. Take time to plan. Sharpen your saw before you try to cut with it. Think a minute about why you are doing something, as well as how you are going to do it.

A high percentage of us are chronically dehydrated simply because we get out of the habit (or never got into it in the first place) of drinking water. And people who are in chronic ruts or routines are people who have gotten out of the habit of thinking. The days just go by, one blurring into the next, and we end up doing the same things, putting out the same fires, following the same schedule, until we are almost living our lives in a sleep mode. Thought can change all that; a new idea, a new perspective, a new way to do something can wake us up and hydrate our minds.

Challenge yourself a little. Ask "Is this really what I want to do? Is this really the way I want to do it?" Or, if you want to challenge yourself a little more, ask "Is this really what the Lord wants me to do? Is this really the way He wants me to do it?"

What appetite are we overcoming here? On the physical level, the water helps curb and control our appetite for food. On the mental level, more conscious thought helps us to master our appetite for constant action and activity.

Sit there for a moment and think. Don't just do something to be busy or to be active. Do it because you have thought it through and decided to do it, and how to do it, and why you are doing it. We live in a world of frenetic and often frantic activity, and we have been deceived into thinking that resting, waiting, pausing and thinking are forms of laziness (or at least are decreasing our productivity). As with food, the goal is not more quantity, but more quality in the things we choose to do and in how we do them.

The best kind of thought is the unhurried, peaceful, creative thought where you ask yourself questions and let answers come. The kind of hurried, pressure-packed thinking we do sometimes, such as cramming for a test or preparing at the last moment for a meeting or an assignment, is like stuffing yourself when you are hungry. Slower, more aware and more sensitive thinking is like the eat-half diet.

A couple of stories come to mind:

One summer, my family was working together on building a summer cabin. We were not experienced builders, but we had plans and tools and instruction books, and we thought we could do it. We kept making small mistakes because we were rushing into things, anxious to get it built and be finished. The mistakes were making things take twice as long, and we finally realized that the thinking was more important than the doing, and that five minutes of thought often revealed a shortcut or a better way, or gave us a warning about some pitfall we were about to fall into. We developed a simple motto that saved us: "Think three times, measure twice, and build once." It applies to most every aspect of life.

I spend some time each summer in a rural farming area and the goal there is to relax and slow down and think. One of the interesting side benefits of this attitude is that I can do things there on the farm that I never thought I could do–and that I haven't been able to do anywhere else. The hydraulics on the tractor died one summer, and, since I was in the thought mode, I just sat there and looked at it for a half hour or so. I traced the lines with my eyes, seeing what went from where, and trying to understand how the system worked. To my great surprise, I began to understand hydraulic systems just by observing, and I discovered the problem and fixed it myself. I had a similar experience with a sprinkler system and another one with a boat engine. I, who had never fixed anything in my life, fixed some fairly complex things just by thinking!

Remember, as with the water before the meal, it is the sequence that matters. Drinking a glass of water after eating does not do as much good as drinking it before, and thinking about how and why to do something after you did it doesn't do as much good as thinking it through before-hand. And remember, fleeting thoughts do not do as much good as captured thoughts. Like carrying a water bottle around to remind yourself to drink, carry a pen and a notepad or little booklet around with you. Jot down thoughts as you have them. Sit there for a minute and let a thought or an idea develop, and capture it in writing.

EXERCISING THE MIND

Back in Chapter 5, we discussed the importance of finding a form of physical exercise that you love, and challenged you to engage in it at least five times per fortnight. Though it is not directly about food or the appetite for food, exercise is a legitimate part of a physical diet because it uses the food. The food is the input, and the exercise is the output.

Exercise puts the fuel we take in to the good use of building muscle and skill and heart/lung capacity and does not leave fuel for the bad use of adding weight or accumulating fat. In a successful diet, the appetite for output (exercise) balances and harmonizes the appetite for input (food), and both appetites, held in check by each other, work to our benefit.

We all know that the mind needs exercise too, and just as physical exercise tones and tunes the body and keeps excess weight off, so mental exercise tunes and trims the mind and holds at bay the dimming and dulling that can come to an idle or passive mind.

Again, it is about cultivating and controlling an input appetite and an output appetite, and balancing the two of them. Mentally, the input appetite is for awareness, stimulation, information, knowledge, data, understanding, etc. and the output appetite is for accomplishing something or contributing something or impressing someone by turning those inputs into outputs.

On the one side, we should learn to control what kind of inputs we let in. We can monitor ourselves to take into our minds quality rather than junk. On the other side, we should strive not only to keep our minds active and fit, but to control how and to what ends we use our minds and their amazing capacity.

Once again, the physical is truly a type for the mental. Just as we expand muscle and extend our skill and capacity by working out physically, so we enhance our mental faculties by exercising our minds. One who has a physically active job may need less additional exercise, and one who is constantly stimulated and mentally challenged in his job may need less outside or additional mental exercise.

Just as we must find physical exercise that we enjoy if it is to become a consistent and pleasurable habit, so we must engage in types of mental stimulation that we enjoy if they are to become something we gravitate to and do out of love more than out of duty. Crossword or Sudoku puzzles may be pleasurable mental exercise for one, mathematic problems for another, writing historical fiction for one, attending discussion groups for another. We must each find our own combination.

But remember that we are talking about output here. The input of reading or studying or listening to music is like eating–and to say "What I do for mental exercise is to read" is a little like saying "What I do for physical exercise is to eat." Physically, the higher the quality of the "food" the better of course, and appetite control is the key to that quality. Mentally, the higher the quality of what we take in the better, and controlling that appetite is the key to mental input.

However, we must also concern ourselves with the output appetites. If we are using our mind and its capacity only to impress or manipulate others, or if we are spending all our mental energy on work that we dislike, our mental exercise will never stimulate us or balance our other appetites and drive us toward quality.

With the physical diet, we are trying to decrease the quantity and increase the quality of what we eat, and at the same time expand what our bodies can do through good (and loved) exercise as well as through the nourishment that our disciplined eating brings in. With the mental diet we are trying to get rid of mental junk food and bring in wholesome, clear thought–and then use that mental nourishment to apply our minds to work and creativity that we love and that matters.

So, the mental challenge is similar to the physical one. Find a form of output mental exercise (creating or solving something) that you love, and engage in it at least a couple of times a week (or five times per fortnight). Let your own desires, appetites, and likes be your guide. It might be writing poetry or fiction. It might be painting or drawing. It might be logic problems or jigsaw puzzles. It might be songwriting or music performance. The best mental exercise creates or solves as it makes your mind work.

MENTAL FASTING— AND SLOWING

I'm sure the chapter on fasting as part of the physical diet (Chapter 6) was no surprise to you. The physical and dietary benefits of fasting are well established.

Let's think back to Chapter 6 on fasting for a minute. What we said, in essence, was that fasting cleanses the body and increases awareness. So you probably think this chapter will be on the mental and spiritual benefits of physical fasting, right? Well no, not actually. Remember that everything physical, particularly when it comes to dieting, is a type or a "teaching symbol" for a mental or spiritual truth. So what we want to do is compare and learn.

Physically, we fast by not taking nourishment for a period. What is the mental equivalent? We know that both the body and the mind have need for nourishment. The body is nourished by the intake of food, and the mind is nourished by the intake of information, ideas, and insights. Fasting, both physical and mental, is about halting our intake and cutting off our external nourishment for a period so we can turn more within ourselves and be more in touch with our soul and our spirit.

At this point you might say, "Wait a minute, Dr. Bridell. You are comparing physical food to mental thought and knowledge and educa-tion? And you are saying we should fast from thinking? Why would I not want to think? I know I eat too much food, but is there such a thing as too much thought?"

Think about it for a minute (excuse the pun). We don't fast because there is too much food, but because there is too much junk food, and because our systems need to shut down and rest occasionally. Fasting cleans us out and re-sets and recommits us to better quality. Similarly, there are not too many thoughts or too many ideas—just too many junk thoughts and bad ideas; we occasionally need to clean house mentally. By trying not to think for a period—trying to close out all the noisy clamor of the world—we reset our minds toward quality thought and begin to discover the treasures within.

When we are eating, our body has to be busy chewing and digesting and replenishing our systems. Physical fasting is turning off the intake so everything can rest and refresh and restart. When we are inputting data and stimulus and concepts, our mind has to be busy processing and analyzing and remembering them. Mental fasting is to discontinue the intake for a while and let the mind reboot and respond to what is going on inside of it.

So you have probably guessed it by now. Mental fasting is medita-tion. And what is meditation? It is just what we have been saying—shut-ting off the outside stimulus and turning off the normal mental pattern so your brain can stop digesting for a while and just be still and peace-ful and rediscover itself.

There are many meditation techniques, and most of them make it sound and feel much more complicated than it really is. Meditation, best defined, is simply mental fasting—turning off the usual "digestion" of analyzing, concentrating, calculating and processing information and just putting the mind at rest.

You can meditate with a mantra, a sound like "ommm" that you repeat and focus on. You can meditate by breathing deeply and trying to think only about the air going in and out of your lungs. You can medi-tate with the Zen technique of just sitting, quiet and relaxed, and emptying your mind. But let me tell you my favorite way to meditate. It has only three steps:

1. Sit in a comfortable spot and relax. If there is a lot of tension in you, relax your body one part at a time–first your head and neck, then your shoulders, etc.

2. Remind yourself that you exist in the here and now. You are in the present. It has never been this moment before and you have never been exactly here before, so everything is new.

3. Be aware of everything around you and in you. Don't concentrate on anything or analyze anything or try to figure anything out. Just be aware. Be aware of what is inside your body–of your breath, your heart beating, your kidneys filtering your blood, your hair and nails growing slowly, your skin reproducing and replacing its cells. Be aware of everything outside of you–the temperature, the atmospheric pressure, sounds, smells, how the air feels on your skin. Accept everything as it is and simply be aware of it. Use your whole mind for awareness. Don't let it go off on tangents or worries or conclusions. Just be aware.

The physical fasting challenge is one day a month. Since the mind is much, much faster than the body, mental fasting ought to happen more often. Find a little time to meditate every day, even for a couple of minutes, and find a longer time on Sundays, when you can sit for a while and really become comfortable with meditation–when you can be still and know.

There is much more to say on this subject, but I must save some of it for part three, the spiritual diet. Keep in mind that we are still in part two, the mental diet, and that there will be a corresponding spiritual chapter later. In the meantime, learn and enjoy the art of mental fasting, which the world calls meditation.

GIVING BACK—AND KNOWING WHEN YOU HAVE ENOUGH

If you recall, Chapter 7 was a major departure, because with it, the Bridell diet stopped being just about you! If you think back, the Physical diet became different from any and all other diets, because suddenly it was not just about you losing weight; it was also about the needs of other people.

Chapter 7 told you that just eating half was not enough–that it was important to give the half you didn't eat to someone who needed it! And it suggested some simple, inexpensive ways to sponsor a Third-world child or assist in feeding the homeless. At that point, the Bridell diet was about doing the right thing as well as doing the smart thing. It was about helping others as well as helping yourself. It was about some other peoples' need to eat more as well as about your need to eat less.

Stated another way: One reason to eat less is that you don't need that much food, and your body is better off without it. The other reason not to eat so much is that other people are starving and the half you don't eat can feed someone else.

It's the same with all appetites. One reason for controlling them is that you are better off if you do. The other reason is that others can be better off if you consume less–less money, less material, less fossil fuel, less of anything that you don't really need.

Can you feed the world or eradicate hunger by eating less? No. But can you help other individuals by giving away your excess, and in the process feel better about them and about the world and about yourself? Yes.

Can you end the oil shortage or stop poverty or improve the self-image of the universe by consuming less? No. But can you improve the world just a bit and make it a little better place for other people by using less and acquiring less and controlling your appetites for every-thing from material wealth to sex? Yes.

Appetites are all about consumption. In the New Testament, James warns against wanting things for the wrong reason: "that ye may con-sume it upon your lusts" (James 4:3). A "lust" is often nothing more than an uncontrolled appetite. When we want things and consume things simply to satisfy our lusts, we have made a serious error involv-ing a spiritual confusion between means and ends.

If hunger or appetite or lust controls us, then eating, or obtaining, or controlling, or getting things becomes an end in itself, and is often destructive both to others and to ourselves. But when we control our appetite, food is the means to other ends. It gives us the energy to do good and to fulfill our stewardships.

It is the same with all appetites. If we seek wealth as a means to help others and bring about good works, we are in control of that appetite, and we will have the Lord's help. Likewise, we can view our appetite for sex as the means for the end of showing our love and commitment to spouse.

Viewing controlled appetites as the means to good and worthy ends causes us to make good decisions and to appreciate the energy and motivation that appetites give us. And there is pleasure and joy in the means! Everyone knows the old cliche about happiness being in the journey rather than in the destination. Appetites, viewed as the means, become joyful as they lead to worthy ends. I refer once more to Alma's words to his son Shiblon, "See that ye bridle all your passions that ye may be filled with love" (Alma 38:12).

Again the bridle metaphor! The horse is not the end but the means. He is not the destination but the way to get there. But what joy there is in riding him–as long as he is in our control–as long as he is bridled! Slow your appetites, bring them into control, make them work for your efforts to give and to serve. Then we are filled with love. Then we are filled with the Holy Ghost.

The appetite for food is the perfect type for other appetites. We control our food appetite, eat less, and give more. Look at three other appetites as parallels:

1. The appetite for wealth or accumulation. So often, uncontrolled, it involves all taking and no giving. We say "All I want is the land next to mine." But the wanting never stops. We want more and more. What we have is never enough. I repeat e.e. cummings's observation: "More, more, more, more; what are we trying to become, morticians?" Understanding the Bridell diet teaches us that more is not always better, that less is often better. We need to understand the concept of "enough," that things should only be the means to more worthy ends, and that giving what we do not need to others is the key to our joy as well as theirs.

2. The appetite for sex. Do we consume this appetite on our own lusts? Do we think too much about our own needs and pleasure and not enough about our spouse? Can thinking more about giving make sex the means to the end of showing true and deep love?

3. The appetite for independence. What a lust this is! We want financial independence, emotional independence, social independence. We get duped into thinking that needing others is a weakness. In fact, what we should want is interdependence. Financial interdependence is how the world really works–giving and receiving. Emotional and social life is the same. The more we focus on the giving, and on needs rather than wants, the more we control this appetite and the more we find joy. Self-reliance can be good, but only when it is the means to being useful to others and to the Church and to the world.

In this concept lies a good definition for the controlling of appetites. Control is first. Consuming less and less is second. Giving what you do not consume is the third part of the definition. It adds up to a classic win-win situation where you help yourself by helping others. It works on the micro as well as the macro level. If you fast and pay fast offerings and that money helps others, everyone wins. If this country finds ways to conserve energy, we are better off, and so are other countries that need more. If you take your somewhat spoiled and somewhat unappreciative children on a humanitarian expedition to a Third-world village to help dig a well or build a clinic, you save lives over there, and you just may save your own child's spiritual life as he begins to become aware of his blessings and of his abilities to give and to serve.

Real diets—for any of our appetites—are based on the principle that controlling helps us to give, and giving helps us to control.

CHAPTER

THE POETIC PART

What in the world is a "Poetic Diet?" That was the question many readers asked when they saw the subtitle of the Dr. Bridell diet. In Chapter 8, readers got their answer, and even a guarantee that writing poetry would help them lose weight. Back when we were still dealing only with the Physical diet I pointed out that there is a connection between our perception and perspective and our self-discipline. A glutton is not very aware or perceptive. His attention is taken up by fulfilling his appetite. He eats fast. His appetite is in control. One who "sips and savors" takes control of his appetite, "bridles it," if you will, reining it in and using it, at the pace he dictates, for his pleasure and enjoyment. Quality takes over for quantity.

The important thing to realize is that the connection between awareness and appetite control works both ways. When we eat slower and bridle the appetite for food, we become more aware of the taste, texture, and enjoyment of our small, slow bites. And working on awareness and poetic sensitivity slows us down and removes the gluttony. It is the same with all appetites: as we control them and slow them down, we begin to notice more and to appreciate more. Training ourselves to see more and be more aware slows us down and brings the animal instincts into control.

Once again, the appetite for food is the type for other appetites. As we gain the "lightness" of a perceptive, observant attitude, we lose "weight" and become a higher type of being.

I had an aunt who was a somewhat famous poet, and who sought to teach me the tricks of her trade when I was a child. I remember one autumn day she pointed at a bright tree and said, "What do you see?"

"A tree," I answered.

"Yes, but what do you see?" she said.

"Well, I see red and orange leaves."

"Good," she said, "and what else?"

She taught me that day to see the patterns in the bark, the delicate flow in the movement of the branches, the imagined intertwining roots underground that give nourishment and balance. When our conversation was over, I saw the tree in a whole new light. (And both the "whole" and the "light" began to have double meanings). She helped me write a poem about the tree, to capture and remember the new perspectives and the new awareness.

That tree was in our front yard, and I never looked at it the same again. I remember walking past it one day on my way home from sixth grade, and thinking, "That tree is a miracle! It is worth more than our house!" I had learned that the best things in life really are free–free to those who learn to really see them and truly appreciate them.

Amazing benefits come from a more poetic soul. We become: More aware, less gluttonous. More appreciative, less greedy. More interested in aesthetics, less interested in self-gratification.

It is telling that in our fast, competitive, greedy world, the first question we often ask those we meet is "What do you do?"

I would rather ask someone "What do you see?" or "What do you feel?"

Feelings and observations–and joy too for that matter–come in moments. Becoming more aware and more appreciative of those moments of joy is the key to happiness (and perhaps to the mission statement God gave us: "Men [and women] are that they might have joy" (2 Nephi 2:25). Awareness of joyful moments gives us the perspective and peace that allows us to slow down a little and gain better control of the appetites to hurry, to obtain, to win, to control, and to gain power.

The best way I know to increase awareness and appreciation of moments is to try to capture them in small, private poems. It might be just a line or two, and your writing can be completely private. This week's challenge is to create at least one short verse about at least one moment of awareness and joy each day. This kind of writing will do three amazing things for you: 1) Help you remember pleasant moments and thus retain their joy longer, 2) Cause you to look harder for those moments and thus recognize more of them, and 3) Make you more attuned to the quality and the blessings that surround you and thus become less susceptible to the pull of petty, personal appetites.

At the risk of embarrassment (and with gratitude for the anonymity of my pseudonym) let me close this chapter with a few of my own little daily verses, the purpose not being to lay claim to any poetic talent, but rather to show you that it takes no talent to attempt!

Ten eyes, four colors,
Billy's chocolate brown, Tawni's tan/green
Holly's violet blue and the last four, two on each twin,
The color of morning sky.

Morning sleeper, arms flung up overhead
Sweet face of virtue,
Soft snores of peace,
Makes it worth it to get up first.

Grief, heavy and sweet,
Choked with love, bearing down on hope.

Celebrate a life and recommit to more love.

A storm over the lake
The wet smell of sagebrush
Stop, use eyes and nose better for just a minute
Because it's a moment.

Early morning, pastoral summer grass, backlit lawn
Through my own plantation shutters as I
Relearn the book of James
Ahhh, solitary morning devotionals.

The rhythm-laughter of memories
Rubbing the pleasant traction of
Renewed acquaintance.
Just a simple dinner with old friends, years melt away
And friendship remains.

THE MENTAL BRIDLE

Pseudonyms are great, especially when they contain symbols. I became Dr. Bridell simply because the objective of this book is to find the secrets of bridling our appetites and passions. The bridle metaphor, particularly for those of us who love horses, is perfect.

Back in the Physical diet I quoted James who used this bridling metaphor and Alma's wonderful "See that ye bridle your passions that ye may be filled with love" (Alma 38:12). I talked about a horse's dangerous strength and suggested that it would be foolish and cowardly to drug or kill a horse to be sure it will not hurt you—that bridling and careful control is a much wiser a solution.

And so it is with our passions and our appetites. These are not things we should want to kill or to medicate out of our lives. They are not our enemies but our energies. They can be our motivators rather than our masters, and a thrill to ride rather than a threat to ruin.

But only if we use the bridle! Until we put the bit of our own control between the teeth of our urges and instincts, these appetites can injure us, wound our destiny, and throw us off the path of our dreams and our goals.

The last thing we should want to do with our appetite for food, or for sex, or for any of God's gifts is to dull it, subdue it, to tie it up or hobble it so it loses its beauty and strength and passion, or to kill it. (This is why things like vows of celibacy seem to me such tragedies) Rather, we should bridle it, harness it, and control it to work with us and for us instead of on us and against us.

Your brain is the bridle, and your mental commitment to eat half as much and twice as slow is the bit that can gradually come to feel natural and accepted in the mouth.

"Your brain is the bridle." Let's explore that idea further. The brain can control the body just as a bridle controls a horse. Work the metaphor a little deeper: Just having a bridle (or a brain) is not enough. We must learn how to use it to control the horse (appetite). We must practice and learn the skills of riding; we must develop the strength of will that puts us in charge. Then and only then does the horse or the appetite serve us and give us joy.

Each chapter in the physical diet focused on an idea or technique or practice that can give us a better bridle and more skill in using it to control the food appetite. Each of those methods, from sipping and savoring to fasting to poetic awareness, can help us learn to bridle all our other physical and mental appetites as well.

What is at stake? Everything! Without the bridle and the developed skill to use it, we spiral down toward danger and death; with it we climb upward toward the confidence and happiness of a wonderful ride.

With discipline and the will gained through practice and effort, we lift ourselves higher toward peace and joy. Without it, we plummet toward obsessions that lead to addictions and other deep unhappiness. And the difference is the bridle!

A bridle actually has three parts. First, the halter or head harness fits snugly over the horse's head to hold everything in place. Second, the bit goes in the horse's mouth so he can be pulled up short and stopped. Third, the reins allow the rider to turn or direct the horse's action and movement.

Our will and discipline, to be effective, need the same parts. First, we need to understand our appetites so we can fit our discipline to its dimensions. We need to understand the purposes and makeup and best uses of food, wealth, power, sex–of every desire or urge we have, and fit them to what we know of the Lord's will and the purpose of life.

Second, we need to absolutely deny or stop our appetites from pulling us in directions we know are contrary to what is right or good for ourselves and those around us. And third, we need to turn or transform the directions our appetites take us from negative to positive. We need to:

- Turn our passion for food away from gluttony and toward serious interest in nutrition and gourmet enjoyment;
- Turn our sexual desires away from pornography or perversion or selfish gratification toward commitment and fidelity and ultimate oneness with our now or future spouse;
- Turn our materialistic interests from envy or covetousness or greed to unselfish magnifying of stewardships;
- Turn our power appetite from Machiavellian control and domination to win-win interdependence.

Like the little transformer toys that kids play with, which, with a few twists and rotations, go from a man to a spaceship or a race car, we can transform our passions from dangerous (to ourselves and to others) masters to obedient and highly beneficial (and joy-giving) servants.

You already have the bridle. God has given it to each of us just as He has given us the horse. It is up to us to use it. It is up to us to learn to ride!

CHAPTER

REVIEW OF THE PRINCIPLES AND PRACTICES OF THE MENTAL DIET

Let's quickly look back at what we have covered so far in the mental part of the diet. It is important to have the principles and practices well in mind in order to implement both the physical and mental parts of the eat-half diet, and to help prepare us to comprehend the spiritual parts of the diet that are still to come. The following lists come from the concepts and challenges outlined in Chapters 11-19. You may also want to compare these mental principles and practices with the physical principles and practices that were reviewed back in Chapter 10.

Simple Principles of the Mental Diet

1. Active, engaged thinking, about a broad range of ideas and things is good for the brain.
2. Our mental appetites, curiosity, and even our lusts can work for us but often work against us because they do not know when to stop or how to direct themselves.
3. At least half of what we take into our brains is junk which is detrimental rather than beneficial to our minds.
4. By limiting and being discerning about what we let into our

brains, "eating half" as it were, we can gradually gravitate toward thoughts and ideas that are twice as good. (Our minds, denied the addicting junk that surrounds us, will begin to appreciate and even demand a higher quality of thought.)

5. By thinking more deliberately and taking our time on important conclusions and decisions, we cast aside stress and pressure and make fewer mistakes.

6. The more sensual attention we pay to our surroundings, the more interesting and pleasing they become.

7. The most important and most enjoyable things we can think about are our stewardships.

8. Thirsting for the clear light of truth will lead to the gift of discernment.

9. A mind that is full of light and truth will ask for and be satisfied with fewer small-minded stimulations (everything from small talk to mindless television.)

10. Letting the brain have downtime to rest periodically can cleanse and rejuvenate and re-calibrate capacity.

11. Mental and spiritual awareness is heightened and sharpened by meditation.

12. Regulating the "output" of mental exercise (creating, planning, solving) is as important as regulating the input of reading, watching, listening.

13. With some effort and attention, everyone can find a form of mental exercise he or she loves.

14. Mental exercise, because of the endorphins it produces, can become a pleasurable positive habit.

15. Service and giving to others take our minds off ourselves and increase our JQ (Joy Quotient) as well as our IQ.

16. Poetry or other artistic outlets enhance awareness, slow us down, orient us to quality, and increase our discipline.

17. The horse and bridle metaphor can help us visualize and implement better control of all of our appetites.

Simple Practices of the Mental Diet

1. Focus on your three stewardships: your family, your work, and yourself (i.e. your character).

2. Mentally create a "choose-to-do" for each of these three stewardships every day–something you don't have to do, but choose to do for the benefit of that stewardship. Plan these before the "have-to-do" list.

3. Slow down. Walk slower, eat slower, think more about what you are feeling, and be consciously aware of each of your five senses and what they are telling you.

4. Visualize. Create things mentally before you do them.

5. Stop thinking and doing once in a while. Just relax, do nothing, think nothing. Take naps. Push your reset button.

6. Exercise your mind through creating or solving. Paint, write, do crosswords or engage in the mental exercise of your choice three times a week.

7. Conserve resources, don't waste, and find a service project or charity that you become passionate about.

Now the same question as on the Physical diet principles and practices: Do you believe these 17 principles? Can you implement these seven practices? Let your belief in the principles expand your motivation to implement the practices.

Work at it! Don't give up! The Mental results will be as obvious as the Physical results of the eat-half diet.

It is fortunate that we use the same word for the losing of weight and for the gaining of illumination, because it enables me to end this section of the book with a single promise that comes to those who implement the Physical diet and to those who implement the Mental diet. The promise is "You will become lighter!"

SECOND INTERMISSION

GIVING FREE REIN TO OUR SPIRITS

Think of this little section as an "intermission" between the Mental and the Spiritual parts of the Bridell diet. In it, we will review where we have been so far and look forward toward the final third of the diet, contained in the next ten chapters.

The first ten chapters laid out the Physical eat-half diet. Based on extensive feedback from the thousands who have tried it, different individuals found different ways to get into the diet. Some found the "sip and savor" approach appealing, others liked the "give back" or "water first" or "poetry" techniques. But the point is, it works. As you see in the testimonials at the front and end of this book, Bridell dieters get weight loss results!

But the promise of the diet is more than physical, more than the loss of weight. The promise is that you will be "lighter" not only in terms of weight but in terms of illumination and optimism–lighter in mind and in mood as well as in body. We moved on, in the next ten chapters, to the Mental diet, applying every type learned from the Physical diet to the way we think and the way we live as well as to the way we eat.

Much of the Mental diet has been the realization that awareness and perspective can lift us above our urges and appetites. The more aware we are, the less greedy we become. The broader our perspective, the less gluttonous we are.

It was Christ, of course, who taught us to elevate all truth and all commandments from the physical to the mental. In place of "don't kill," He said "don't be angry." And instead of "don't commit adultery," He said "don't lust."

Essentially then, physical appetites are controlled with mental attitudes and disciplines. If we sip and savor, concentrating (with our minds) on the taste and joy and quality of eating, we bring the physical appetite to eat under our mental control. The horse and bridle metaphor works at every level. By bridling the horse's head, we control his body.

The apostle James put it perfectly: "Behold, we put bits in the horses' mouths, that they may obey us; and we turn about their whole body" (James 3:3).

The problem is that physical appetites are not the only ones we have. There are also social/emotional/mental appetites, lusts, and passions that can destroy us if we let them have their way and take control of our lives. They can work for us or against us depending on which way we lead them.

So here is the question: If our mental faculties can bridle and control the physical appetites, what is it that can bridle and control the mental appetites? The answer, of course, is the spiritual. Just as we must elevate our physical appetites to the mental level in order to bridle them, we must elevate our mental appetites to the spiritual level in order to bridle them.

These three levels represent three completely different ways of thinking and of being. When we live on the physical level, we are animals—obeying our instincts, appetites, urges and lusts, and following the law of the jungle. When we live on the mental level, we are rational, decision-making human beings—analyzing, making conscious choices based on what we think is good and what we think makes sense, and following the laws of logic and of men. When we live on the spiritual level, we are children of God—seeking His will, tapping into His power, striving to do what is right and what is His will, and living by His law.

Even if you know that you exist on all three planes, physical, mental, and spiritual, it is not easy to elevate yourself up to the higher levels. When you look at another person, what do you see, what do you perceive, what are you interested in? Are you inclined to see a person's body and appearance, or his mind, or his spirit? Oh, that we could see the spirit more easily. The standard greeting in India is "Namaste," which, literally translated, means "I see the divine spark within you"? Oh, that we really could see that part of each person we meet.

Appetites can be identified and classified, and potentially controlled, on the same three physical, mental, and spiritual levels. Physical appetites such as food and sex, when they are left to the physical, become gluttony and perversion. When they are bridled by the mental, they provide us with nourishment and allow us to express love and joy.

Mental/emotional/social appetites (such as those for power, control, popularity, and wealth), if they are given their head, can run away to selfish obsessions for dominion, materialism, and fame—or, they can be bridled and transformed to the spiritual desire for stewardship, wisdom, contribution and discipleship.

So here is the secret: Spiritual appetites are all good. True spiritual desires are all for aspects and dimensions of the Lord's will. Spiritual appetites are for truth, wisdom, faith, insight, righteousness, and for eternal awareness, perspective, and connections.

Unlike physical appetites (which, unchecked, will always harm us) and mental appetites (which can result in bad or good depending on our skill with the bridle), spiritual appetites (the urges and longings and desires of our spirits) all draw us to Home and to God. The trick (and the ultimate goal of the Bridell diet) is first to put the physical under the control of the mental bridle, and then to transform our mental appetites into spiritual ones, where the bridle becomes the will of God's mind rather than of our own.

During the course of the next ten chapters, we will progress and elevate to the Spiritual diet. But as we do, remember that the benefits and dividends are still physical and mental as well. The better you get at the Mental and Spiritual diets, the more you will control your physical weight. The principles remain the same on all levels. And the techniques and control methods you have learned and continue to practice for the food diet are good training as well as good metaphors for the mental and spiritual diets.

Actually, developing and honing your positive and beneficial spiritual appetites gives you the ultimate control of your negative and potentially harmful physical and mental appetites. Remember this as we shift paradigms in the next ten chapters: The Spiritual diet is more than a better bridle, it is a shift of horses. And the Spiritual horse, you see, does not need a bridle at all. It is a horse you can trust, a horse that knows the way Home. It is a horse that was sent to you, and that can transform its rider to resemble its Sender.

THE SPIRITUAL DIET

FOCUSING ON GOD'S WILL—
CHOOSING HIS HALF

The intermission you have just read compared the Spiritual diet to a shift of horses. Most horses need a bridle to keep them in check, but the Spiritual horse needs no bridle at all because you can trust it to know the way Home. Not only that, I said it was sent to you, and can transform you to resemble its Sender.

Although this terminology may sound a bit strange, the basic spiritual appetite is to discover and do God's will. The spirit in each of us is drawn toward Home and toward light. Yet that spirit is encased in a mortal body which, according to God's plan, is filled with physical and mental/emotional appetites that, if unbridled, pull us in other directions. Thus our mortality is subject to the tugs and forces of the opposing, dark side.

Bridling these mortal appetites and pulling them into control can fill us with strengthening love that enables us to catch up to and ultimately swing across and mount the spiritual horse. Doing this is both the test and the glorifying challenge of life on this earth.

Mortality really offers, ultimately, only two basic choices: Light or darkness. Each choice moves us either toward God or away from Him.

Everything that entices us to good is from Him (see Alma 5:40.). Everything that leads us away is not. The spiritual eat-half diet consists simply of choosing His half of life, of behavior, of being!

This is a huge paradigm shift. In the Physical and Mental diet, the challenge was to control our urges and our appetites. In the Spiritual diet, the challenge is to give control to Him. In the ultimate spiritual reality, the only thing we have to give to God is our agency. When we truly and fully do that, we have relinquished all control–no longer needing the bridle, because we have climbed on a very different kind of horse which, unbridled, takes us always in His direction.

The physical and mental horses still live in our pasture, and we must ride them too because we own them, and we love them, and we appreciate what they can do for us. We ride them always with a bridle, and always in control, and we are filled with more and more love. Over time they become better and more manageable horses because they are ridden well and because they share the same pasture with the Spiritual horse (which we do not own, but over which we are stewards).

It is hard to know the right name for this total paradigm shift onto the third horse. Submission? Consecration? Whatever it is, it changes everything. We move directly away from self-determination and control–the very things the whole world seems to be seeking. Compare the oft quoted "Invictus," written in the 19th century, with the rebuttal of early Church Apostle Orson Whitney. These two poems explain the concept better than I could with logic and prose:

Invictus by William E. Henley
Out of the night that covers me,
Black as the Pit from pole to pole,
I thank whatever gods may be
For my unconquerable soul.

In the fell clutch of circumstance,
I have not winced nor cried aloud.
Under the bludgeonings of chance

My head is bloody, but unbowed.

Beyond this place of wrath and tears
Looms but the Horror of the shade,
And yet the menace of the years
Finds, and shall find, me unafraid.

It matters not how strait the gate,
How charged with punishments the scroll,
I am the master of my fate:
I am the captain of my soul.[5]

**The Soul's Captain [The Answer] by Elder Orson F. Whitney
of the Quorum of the Twelve**
Art thou in truth? Then what of him
Who bought thee with his blood?
Who plunged into devouring seas
And snatched thee from the flood?

Who bore for all our fallen race
What none but him could bear.
The God who died that man might live,
And endless glory share?

Of what avail thy vaunted strength,
Apart from his vast might?
Pray that his Light may pierce the gloom,
That thou mayest see aright.

Men are as bubbles on the wave,
As leaves upon the tree.
Thou, captain of thy soul, forsooth
Who gave that place to thee?
Free will is thine–free agency

To wield for right or wrong;
But thou must answer unto him
To whom all souls belong.

Bend to the dust that head "unbowed,"
Small part of Life's great whole!
And see in him, and him alone,
The Captain of thy soul.[6]

Oh, what folly to believe we are the captains, to think we have any real control. We have been bought by Him who has all control, and in this we should find our greatest rejoicing. What errors we would make if we were really in charge–mistakes that might rob us of the very things we were sent here to gain.

The eat-half diet, in its spiritual phase, becomes the choose-half diet. We choose His half, we choose the Light. What we give away is the dark half, the natural man, the world. And we give to Him the only thing we really have, the only thing we can even claim to own, our agency!

In the next chapter, we will explore further how obsession with control can suck the quality and the joy out of our lives, and make us forget the true Captain of our souls. And we will think more about the magnificent and adventuresome ride we are in for as we give the Spiritual horse his head and commit ourselves to going wherever He takes us.

WHAT SLOWING DOWN AND TUNING YOUR SPIRIT WILL DO FOR YOU

Let me begin with a feedback letter I received:

Dr. Bridell,

Wanted you to know how well your diet works and the freedom it provides. I was on my way to the doctor to look into gastric bypass. I was that desperately crazy. I talked at length with my long-ago visiting teacher who is now a long-distance friend and she said to look into your "mysterious" diet. It works, she said. And so it does.

In five months I am down over 90 pounds–40 to go. I have not suffered. I have changed little, but then I have changed everything about how I eat. Half of everything, lots of water, swimming because I love to and I do not care how I look in a bathing suit, walks when I want to, which have turned into daily. (My chocolate lab has lost 10 pounds, which she needed to do.) My husband has Parkinson's disease and he is now much healthier because he is along for the ride, as he says. The Word of Wisdom has taken on new meaning for me and my husband. Scriptures every morning (a habit I had skipped), prayer all the time–and so much more. It works. It is wonderful. Thank you so much for restoring my spirit through your "mysterious" self.

A friend, admirer and more
Shalom
JC

I wanted to share this letter because it provides an interesting segue between the Physical/mental diets and the Spiritual one. This reader, in addition to her dramatic physical results, has been invited by the diet to a more spiritual place where scripture and prayer and all things of the Spirit have become more prominent–higher on her priority list.

The promise of the Physical diet (Chapter 2) is that as you cut the quantity intake of food by half, your body will start desiring and demanding better quality in what you do put in your mouth. Junk and fast food will look less appetizing; vegetables and fruit will look better and better. Remember, the same principle works with your mind (chapter 12). As you cut some of the trash and non-nourishing media stuff out of your life, your mind will gradually begin to appreciate and even crave more quality in your activities, your entertainment, your interests, and your relationships.

In the Physical diet, the key to eating half as much is to eat twice as slow. Slow down the way you eat (smaller bites, more chewing, savoring each morsel), and your body rewards you by enjoying food more, craving quality, and getting fitter and stronger. In life we need to do the same thing. As you slow down and simplify the way you live and the way you think, your brain rewards you by producing better ideas and purer thoughts, noticing more beauty, and becoming more perceptive and more aware.

We talked about comparing all the appetites to interlocking gears with the "drive gear" the appetite for hurry, haste, speed which feeds each of our appetites and lets all of them pull harder on us. I explained that slowing down any of the interlocking gears can begin to slow them all down, and that slowing down our eating is a good place to start. When we sip, smell, and savor we change the unhealthy rush of quick-quantity refueling to a pleasurable tasting of quality. The very process of slowing down that gear begins to slow down the others. We taste, and while we are tasting, we start seeing more and hearing more, and thinking more. I said, "Let that kiss for your loved one take a little longer. Look into a person's eyes and hold their hand a half second longer when you greet someone. Sit down and take a look around you for a moment before you start a piece of work."

Do you begin to see the pattern? Slowing down physically produces mental benefits, and, likewise, slowing down mentally produces spiritual blessings. Slowing down our body helps us control physical appetites; we lose weight and become more cerebral, our minds more alert and more alive. Slowing down our brains clarifies and sharpens our thoughts and opens up the space and the channels into which and through which inspiration and spiritual nourishment flows.

The scriptures say, "Be still and know that I am God" (Psalm 46:10). The simple fact is that inspiration and enlightenment cannot come to a hurried, frazzled, multi-focused mind. Quieting the mind, slowing it down, and making it still and receptive is the key to inviting and feeling the Spirit.

The hectic world we live in today is the hardest environment there has ever been for that kind of slowing and stillness. All of our senses are almost constantly bombarded–by noise, by lights, by commercial messages, by endless information that exceeds by a million times what we could ever take in. Nature and the quiet countryside which inspired and nourished our grandparents is virtually gone, replaced with a "virtual reality" so superficial that it reflects away rather than absorbing in the Spirit.

Yet the Spirit, when it is within us, somehow holds the swirling stress at bay, and creates within us an island of calm awareness. Parley P. Pratt in his book Science, the Key to Theology, described the effects of the Spirit as a gift that "adapts itself to all the organs and attributes. It quickens all the intellectual faculties, increases, enlarges, expands and purifies all the natural passions and affections; and adapts them, by the gift of wisdom, to their lawful use. It inspires, develops, cultivates and matures all the fine-toned sympathies, joys, tastes, kindred feelings and affections of our nature. It inspires virtue, kindness, goodness, tenderness, gentleness and charity. It develops beauty of person, form and features. It tends to health, vigor, animation and social feeling. It invigorates all the faculties of the physical and intellectual man. It strengthens, and gives tone to the nerves. In short, it is, as it were, marrow to the bone, joy to the heart, light to the eyes, music to the ears, and life to the whole being."[7]

Quite a gift! So let's ask the chicken and egg question: Does the Spirit calm us and clear us and slow us, or does our own slow, still calm attract the Spirit to us? The answer is that it works both ways!

Our physical, mental and spiritual parts have profound effect on each other. If we rush and hurry physically, we stress and frazzle our thought process, making it erratic and scattered. And vice versa. A frantic physical and mental pace creates within us a scattered, unreceptive spirit. And vice versa.

But when we consciously slow ourselves down, body and mind, moving slower, thinking more deliberately, finding some time and place for solitude, the Spirit finds us more easily and dwells with us. And when we pray for and feel the Spirit, it slows us down, makes us more aware, transforms physical/mental appetites to spiritual ones which lift us toward God rather than pulling us down and away.

So besides eating slower, moving slower, and thinking more deliberately, we want to make a conscious effort to pray slower (listening more, thinking more), to breathe and meditate more deeply, to read one verse of scripture but think about it as long as it would normally take us to read ten. In other words, do the spiritual things slower just as you slow down the physical and the mental.

When you bridle and control and slow down the body, it rewards you by shedding unwanted weight and by beginning to crave good things rather than junk. When you bridle the mind, it rewards you by becoming more discerning and more creative and by gravitating to the light. And when you care for and focus on the needs of your spirit, taking time to listen while you pray and to "wait upon the Lord," your spirit rewards you by connecting to the Spirit and causing you to desire what He desires for you.

CHAPTER

SPIRITUAL SIPPING AND SAVORING

Thinking back to the corresponding Physical and Mental chapters (3 and 13) you will remember these principles: When our food appetite controls us, we rush through meals, gorging ourselves, animal-like, and miss much of the taste and enjoyment. When our other appetites, lusts, and instincts control us (particularly the pervasive appetite for hurry and haste), we rush through our days, missing much of the beauty and subtlety that makes life worth living.

When we control our food appetite, sipping, smelling, and savoring our food rather than gorging, gulping, and guzzling it, we can appreciate and taste every morsel. When we control our other appetites (for work, for control, for instant gratification, and especially for haste) we begin to find the moments of joy that are the very purpose of life.

In those earlier chapters, I said, "Some people can induce an inner calm simply by commanding themselves to slow down (eating slower, walking slower, etc). Others, like a horse straining at the bit, become more jumpy and anxious when forced to go slower. The key for this second type of person is to focus on awareness instead of on slowing down . . . In other words, sip, smell, and savor your life rather than gorging, gulping and guzzling it."

As with every other aspect of this diet, and every aspect of our appetites, the physical (and the food) serves as a type that helps us better understand, control, and bridle all other instincts, urges and desires. Once again, as we bridle the physical and the mental, we get to the point where we can develop the beneficial spiritual appetite that needs no bridling and that draws us closer to God.

So, how does one apply the principle of sip, smell and savor to spiritual things? Some applications are clear: Sip the scriptures, read one verse or one phrase and dwell on it, let it come alive, giving the Spirit time to open it to your spirit. "Smell" and feel the presence of the Spirit and be aware of its calming influence. Savor your prayers, taking time to listen and find the power of two-way communication with Heavenly Father.

Other applications may be less obvious: One who sips and savors is one who appreciates and loves what he receives. Becoming a good receiver of the gifts of God is a rare skill. We are so busy doing and being and giving (all good things) that we don't have much time or thought left over to simply receive.

We live at the best time, in the best place, and under the best circumstances of anyone who has ever lived. Most of us live in a land of freedom and enjoy the truths of the Restored Gospel. And yet we may not fully receive these gifts and are not fully grateful for them. "Taking for granted" is the opposite of being a great and grateful receiver. We can develop a wonderful spiritual appetite for thankfulness and for awareness of all that we receive.

When we slow down and sip and savor our food, we receive the gift of taste and enjoyment. When we slow down other appetites and urges and become more observant mentally and more sensitive to the beauty and the people around us, we receive the gift of added awareness and perspective which enhances our joy.

And when we slow down and find the Spirit's rhythm in our prayers, our scripture study, our meditation, our worship, and our gratitude, we receive the gift of discernment, which is one of the great and powerful gifts of God. It can protect us, it can reveal to us the nature and receptivity of the spirits of others, and it can help us make good choices and decisions.

Remember again what Lehi taught his son Jacob (and the rest of us) "Adam fell that man might be [mortal]; and men are [mortal], that they might have joy" (2 Nephi 2:25). Joy comes in moments, and those moments of joy can come with more frequency and more intensity when we learn to slow down and appreciate and savor the things around us.

CHAPTER

LIVING WATER

One of the really wonderful stories of the New Testament is of the Savior and the woman at the well. I love His statements that "if thou knewest the gift of God and who it is that saith to thee, Give me to drink; thou wouldest have asked of him, and he would have given thee living water" (John 4:10) and that "whosoever drinketh of the water that I shall give him shall never thirst; but the water that I shall give him shall be in him a well of water springing up into everlasting life" (John 4:14).

What is living water, and how do we obtain it? To try to get the answer to that spiritual question, let's review the role of water in the physical and mental diets, remembering Chapters 4 and 14.

"Chronically dehydrated people (a high percentage of us) get out of the habit of drinking water. And people who are in chronic ruts or routines are people who have gotten out of the habit of thinking. Thought can change it; a new idea, a new perspective, a new way to do something can wake us up and hydrate our minds. . . . clear water is replaced by clear thought, and the habit we need to develop is to always drink in some pure thought before we shift into eating away at any kind of action."

So now that we are into the Spiritual diet, consider this: How many of us are experiencing "Chronic Spiritual Dehydration?" Like water, we need spiritual nourishment constantly, consistently. We need more of it than we will get if we wait to drink until we are extremely or noticeably thirsty.

Perhaps praying fervently only in crisis or times of deep need is like drinking only when extremely thirsty. Perhaps reading a verse of scripture routinely or robotically once a day is more like taking medicine, one pill a day, than like really drinking in the scriptures.

The scriptures not only talk about the need for spiritual nourishment; they advocate thirsting for righteousness, and thirsting to become like God.

Thirst is an appetite, and spiritual thirsting is a spiritual appetite which, like all spiritual appetites, benefits us and needs no bridling. How do we develop and encourage this spiritual thirst, and what is the living water to which it should be directed?

Spiritual water is the Gospel and the Atonement, and we drink it in by accepting it and by desiring it. Spiritual water is feeling the presence of the Lord. Spiritual hydration comes from having the Holy Ghost in us, coursing through us, refreshing and renewing us.

Just as drinking a full glass of water before eating controls and limits what we eat, drinking in the Spirit before the consumption of the day can control and limit what we take into our minds and our souls as the day progresses. By taking in the good first, we do not want the bad.

The spiritual application is clear isn't it? Clear but not easy! It amounts to developing our spiritual appetite and prioritizing it above and before our physical and mental appetites. Here is the application: Before you eat physical food or consume mental food, take a long drink of spiritual, living water. Have your personal prayer and read the scriptures before you eat anything in the morning. Drink the spiritual prayer and scripture before you turn on the T.V. or read the newspaper or take in any mental food. Doing so will cause you to want less of the world and to want to select the best things from the world.

There is another application or type that we can take from the

Physical diet. Earlier, we said that more water really is the perfect complement to less food all day long. If you get a good water bottle that you like the look and feel of, and carry it around with you, sipping becomes a good habit.

Do something similar spiritually. Get a small book of scripture that you like the look and feel of, and carry it around with you. Have it with you in the car, set it on your desk, keep it near you. Let opening it become a habit. I like to do it by seasons. In the winter, I carry an Old Testament, in the spring, I carry the New Testament, in the summer I carry the D&C, and in the fall, I carry the Book of Mormon. (I like the small volumes that fit in a purse or briefcase.)

Water –physical water, mental water, and spiritual (living) water–is a huge key to the Bridell diet. Love it! Drink it! Get results!

EXERCISING FAITH

In the Physical diet, it was obvious that exercise had to be an integral part of losing weight and staying fit. Clearly, we have to pay attention to the "output" of exercise as well as to the "intake" of food. The Mental diet also carries the obvious need of exercise for the brain.

Applying this principle to the Spiritual diet is made easy by the wording in many of our sacred books. Think about the terminology of scripture, and its use of the metaphors of exercise and exertion and training and discipline:

- "Wrestle with the Spirit" (Enos !:2)
- "Exercise Faith" (Alma 26:22)
- "And they did wax stronger and stronger and firmer and firmer" (Helaman 3:35)
- "Pray with all the energy of your heart" (Moroni 7:48)
- "Pray morning, noon and night." (Psalm 55:17)

It is abundantly and scripturally clear that exertion, regularity, and discipline are required as much in spiritual progression as in physical or mental training.

I am reminded of a recently returned missionary who said, "I just can't seem to get in the Spirit like I did on my mission." It was then pointed out to him that on the mission he read the scriptures intently for at least a half hour every morning and prayed hard at least three times a day. Just as a casual toss of a ball a couple of times or a leisurely trot around a track once in a while will never get your body in shape (or cause any weight loss), so a brief perfunctory prayer now and then or one quick verse of scripture will not bring us into sound and tuned spiritual shape (or cause any positive change from the mindsets and attitudes of the world).

Serious training is all about intensity of effort and regularity and discipline of exercise. But more than that, as we emphasized with the physical and mental, it is about finding a form of exercise that you love, so that you do it because you want to, not just because you should.

So here are two challenges:

1. Pray and read scripture with regularity and intensity. Pray morning noon and night, and focus the energy of your heart and the intensity of your mind as you do. Kneel. Apply your energy to your prayer. Take notes on any answers or impressions that come. Will your spirit to make a real connection with the Spirit as you pray. Also, concentrate hard on the scriptures at least once a day. Read what you read with avid interest. After all, what is more important?

2. Find a new and more exciting way to pray and study scripture that you love. Try different things. Read by subject or by research topic rather than chronologically. Read early in the morning or after lunch or some different time than usual. Read from a different book of scripture each month or each season. Read with a friend on the phone. Find a new and beautiful location in which to read. Sing a hymn from the hymnbook and then read the two scriptures at the bottom of the page that go with that hymn. Pray right after physical exercise when your mind is alert. Pray in your closet (literally, if your closet is big enough) or find another quiet, private place. Pray aloud with your spouse where either of you can say what comes to mind within the same prayer rather than only one of you being voice. Pray in your fields. Pray while you

drive. Pray out loud. Pray sometimes in thoughts rather than words. Keep trying new ways of praying and find the ones you love most, the ones that work best for you.

I have a friend who says "There is nothing better than a physical workout. The endorphins get flowing, the blood is pumping, and you feel so great." I agree and disagree. I agree it feels great, but I disagree that nothing feels better. The fact is there is nothing better than a spiritual workout. The Spirit gets flowing, and you feel His love.

FASTING AND SLOWING
AND FEASTING

In the mental diet, we compared physical fasting with mental fasting. In Chapter 16, I said: "Everything physical, particularly when it comes to dieting, is a type or a "teaching symbol" for a mental or spiritual truth. . . Fasting, both physical and mental, is about halting our intake and cutting off our external nourishment for a period so that we can turn more within ourselves and be more in touch with our soul and our spirit. Both physical and mental fasting (meditation) produce an ironic slowing of the mind and spirit that is conducive to inspiration. During a fast one feels less nervous energy, less tendency to rush or to worry about detail. It somehow becomes easier to have perspective, to see the big picture, to focus in on what really matters. And as this happens, time seems to slow down."

While we must bridle and control and often deny our physical and mental appetites, remember that all spiritual appetites draw us to Heaven; they do not need a bridle, because they are a horse that we can trust and that will lead us back to God. So, if the spiritual dimension of each aspect of the diet is the opposite of the physical and the mental, it shouldn't be surprising that the spiritual equivalent of fasting is feasting. It is feasting on the word. It is feasting on the goodness and generosity and gifts of God, and on the richness and wonder of the Spirit.

In the Physical and Mental diets, we stop our intake (of food or of thought) so that we can clear our bodies and our heads. The fasting and the meditation slow us down and tune us in. But tunes us in for what? For the Spiritual feast! In the Spiritual diet we need to do just the opposite: stop our output and increase our intake. Stop doing for a bit and focus on receiving.

In prayer, we can have a spiritual fast/feast by curtailing our output of asking/requesting/pleading for a while, and focus on the intake of listening/receiving/thanksgiving. Feast on the blessings you already have. Consume them by appreciating them. Praise God for His goodness in giving them to you. Feast on your spiritual bounty.

At least once a week, have a special, private personal prayer that lasts at least ten full minutes where you ask for nothing, rather you just thank God for all you have, feasting on His blessings. And during your normal prayers, focus on listening more (receiving prompts and impressions and answers, being silent, waiting for insights on the things you have asked). Be silent, in the receiving mode for at least as much of the prayer as you are speaking, in the asking mode.

The real benefits come when the Physical, Mental, and Spiritual diets are practiced together. It is certainly true with this fasting/slowing principle. As we fast physically, the body benefits through weight loss and system clearing, the mind becomes clearer, and the spirit becomes more receptive. As we fast mentally (meditation) the body relaxes, the mind re-sets, and the spirit opens up to the Spirit. And as we feast spiritually, the body is renewed, the mind quickened, and the spirit reborn. We receive these blessings as we apply the principles of fasting/slowing to our bodies, our minds, and our spirits–in other words, to our souls.

CHAPTER

THE SPIRITUAL APPETITE
FOR GIVING AND SERVING

In earlier chapters, we established the interesting relationship between controlling our consumption and giving to others. In the Physical diet, when we got to this giving part, the paradigm shifted, and suddenly we were talking not only about caring for our own bodies, but about caring about the bodies of others. In the mental diet, we began to see that a key reason for controlling all of our appetites is that it increases both our capacity and our motivation to care more and to love more. I said, "When we control our appetite, food is the means to other ends. It gives us the energy to do good and to fulfill our stewardships. It is the same with all appetites. If we seek wealth as a means to help others and bring about good works, we are in control of that appetite, and we will have the Lord's help. Likewise, we can view our appetite for sex as the means for the end of showing our love and commitment to spouse."

The lesson we learned with regard to physical and mental appetites is that they must be controlled; that when they are, we give ourselves a gift and, at the same time, put ourselves in a position to give gifts to others. The question is, does it work the same way with spiritual appetites?

The key in answering is to remember that physical and mental appetites are the appetites of mortality—of our physical bodies and brains. They will destroy us if they are not controlled, but exalt us if they are. These "horses" must be bridled.

Spiritual appetites on the other hand, are the appetites of eternity, and they save rather than destroy. They are a new kind of horse that needs no bridle and that will take us Home. Spiritual appetites come from God and are of God and can make us like God. They are appetites or desires for all He has: for wisdom and knowledge, for faith and for peace, for love and for service. Spiritual passions must be developed and magnified, not controlled or bridled.

Spiritual appetites are as different as the loaves and fishes of the Lord were from ordinary food. While ordinary food diminishes and disappears as it is consumed, spiritual food multiplies and increases as it is consumed, and as it is given away!

On the spiritual level, giving becomes giving back. We know that we have been given everything by God, so when we pay our tithing, we are simply returning ten percent to Him. When we help or serve in any way, we are simply giving back a tiny morsel of what He has given us.

Giving thus becomes easier, and the more we give, the more we seem to have. In the physical and mental paradigms, we often experience the "scarcity mentality" where giving to someone else subtracts from what we have. However, in the spiritual paradigm, we can experience the "abundant mentality" where giving always adds to what we have. As His servants, it is natural to want to give His gifts. We represent Him when we help and serve and give to others.

With a mental or physical appetite, we often find that the more we eat, the more we want, and we move toward addiction. With the spiritual appetite to give and to serve, we learn a new type of positive habit. The more we serve the more we wish to serve and the more blessings we receive. Spiritual appetites turn us outward rather than inward and somehow, the more we give the more we get and the leaner and stronger and more "tuned" we become. The unselfishness of spiritual appetites, particularly the appetite to give and to serve, often overrides the very kind of selfish physical and the mental appetites that make us greedy, self-centered, and fat.

In *The Lion, the Witch and the Wardrobe,* the children become so devoted and tuned in to Aslan, that author C.S. Lewis says they want to be eaten by him, to be swallowed up in His will. Our spiritual appetites are not to eat, but to be eaten–to become a part of Christ and His work, to do His will, to become more like Him, and to serve Him by serving as He served.

Service brings His peace. Giving takes our minds off ourselves and our wants and selfish appetites. When we develop and expand our unselfish spiritual appetites, we have an easier time controlling the selfish appetites of our bodies and minds.

SPIRITUAL POETRY

Back in the corresponding Physical and Mental chapters (8 and18) we discussed the connections between awareness and discipline and about how attempts to see and observe like a poet can help us be more aware of (and thus more careful about) the quality of what we are taking into our bodies and our minds.

The important thing to realize is that the connection between awareness and appetite control works both ways. When we eat slower and bridle the appetite for food, we become more aware of the taste, texture, and enjoyment of our small, slow bites. Increasing our awareness and poetic sensitivity slows us down and gives us more control of our urges. It is the same with all appetites. As we bridle them and slow them down, we begin to notice more and appreciate more.

Because it seems so relevant, I keep thinking of the common greeting in India. In place of "hello" or "how are you" they say, "Namaste," which, literally translated, means, "I see the divine spark within you." What a great way to greet a person! And what a fantastic way to view people. In a world caught up with fashion and outward appearance, what a powerful perspective to see the spirit of another person rather than just his or her body or physical form.

The reason poetry is important to the Physical and Mental diets is that it causes us to have increased awareness, which lifts us to a higher realm of thought and places us above and in control of our appetites. But with the physical and mental, we are talking about the awareness of our senses—about what we can notice and be aware of via sight, sound, taste, touch, smell, and feelings.

Spiritual awareness and perspective, on the other hand, comes from different sources and is far more insightful and transcending. As we increase our spiritual perspective and awareness we can literally lift ourselves out of the physical and view our body and our mind as tools that our spirits can use. Physical appetites, in this context, are simply one part of our bodily tool, one aspect over which our spirits have control. The shape and weight of that physical tool is then at the command of the spirit.

Spiritual awareness and perspective is actually, in and of itself, a spiritual appetite, one of those marvelous, higher type of appetites in regard to which we can never have too much, and for which we need no bridle or discipline. But it is an acquired appetite, one we have to cultivate and develop.

We need, first of all to be convinced that seeing people (or things or situations) spiritually is more interesting and more enjoyable than seeing them physically. We have to truly believe that the attractiveness of a person's spirit is more important than the attractiveness of his or her body. And we have to really want to see our unfolding lives and the lives of others, as the unfolding of God's plan rather than as mere chance or circumstance.

Poetry was suggested as a tool for increasing sensory awareness. Could it help with spiritual awareness? Certainly there is such a thing as spiritual poetry or as poems about spiritual things; trying to write that kind of poem could certainly enhance our spiritual awareness. But I think there are some even better ways. Let me give you three challenges, each of which will increase and magnify your spiritual perspective and awareness. Think of them as "spiritual poetry."

1. Take "prayer notes." Have a pad and a pen in your hands as you pray. Ask and listen. Pause and wait. Open your mind and your spirit to impressions and answers. Take notes on what you receive. Any impressions that come during earnest prayer are spiritual awareness.

2. Keep an "ask journal." When you ask God for something, write it down and keep track of it along with any nudges or impressions that come to you as you are asking for it. The impressions may alter or edit what you ask for. Look back over past entries often and be aware of how the answers are coming.

3. Ask for "Namaste." Directly ask God to help you to see people's spirits and to be aware of their hearts. Ask to see their divine spark and to see them a little more as God sees them. Ask that this extra perceptively also apply to how you see yourself.

It has been said that the difference between man and God is awareness and perspective. He is aware of all and sees from every perspective. Enhancing our spiritual awareness and perspective is thus the greatest spiritual appetite, and the most direct route to the goal of eternity—becoming, ever so gradually, more like our Father in Heaven.

THE SPIRITUAL BRIDLE

Back in the Physical and Mental diet sections, we paid homage to James for the bridle metaphor. "We put bits in the horses' mouths," said James, "that they may obey us, and we turn about their whole body" (James 3:3). To become "perfect men," he said, we must be "able also to bridle the whole body" which can include our expressions and our appetites. And I repeat Alma's beautiful and provocative statement to his son Shiblon, "See that ye bridle your passions that ye may be filled with love" (Alma 38:12).

Actually, two great and important ways to control and master our physical and mental appetites make these gifts of mortality work for us rather than against us:

1. Bridle them and hold them in check, making them serve our will and give us joy rather than carrying us away.

2. Cultivate and develop our spiritual appetites to the point that they supersede our physical and mental appetites.

As we have discussed before, our spiritual appetites need no bridle.

They are a different kind of horse we can totally trust that will always take us home. (You horse people know that no matter how lost you are, your horse always knows how to get home.)

With spiritual appetites (remember, spiritual appetites are for scripture, prayer, peace, and for insight to the mind and will of God) there is no excess, no way to "gulp and guzzle." Rather, we "feast," and can never reach the point of too much. Obviously, we still need balance in our lives, but we can trust this horse to give us line upon line, to take us as far as we can go on any given day, to take us past, or over, or around, or through whatever dangers or challenges lie in the path.

Remember that the Physical and Mental horses still live in our pasture, and we must ride them too, always with a bridle, and always in control so that they gradually become better and more manageable horses. Somehow though, even as we love and enjoy and use the Mental and Physical horses, we long to spend more and more time riding bareback and without reins or bridle on the Spiritual horse.

Over time, as we nurture and magnify the Spiritual horse, we begin to learn how to become "horse whisperers" who can communicate constantly and with perfect understanding. Unlike the Physical and Mental horses, always kept under our watchful control, the Spiritual horse has complete freedom, because we trust it even more than we trust ourselves. Thus it reveals things to us, drawing us toward its true Owner, and giving us guidance as to how to handle the other two horses.

We learn that if we ride the Spiritual horse first each morning and last each night, the other horses behave better during the day and we sleep better at night. We learn that whenever we are riding the Spiritual horse, the other two follow along obediently, giving us no trouble whatsoever.

We take some criticism for riding the Spiritual horse. Some say we are extremists, and that we are a little strange, like the horse we ride. They say that they are not even sure that what we are riding is a horse, because it looks different and acts differently. Some even make fun of the horse and of us when we are riding it.

We begin to notice that the Spiritual horse really is different, and gradually we realize that it is actually not a horse at all, but a unicorn!

We tell others that and they scoff, assuring us there is no such thing as a unicorn, and that we are only imagining things. "Give up on this crazy idea," they tell us. "There are no unicorns, and if there were, you certainly couldn't ride it bareback, so come back to riding regular horses like the rest of us, and don't be so strict with the bridle. Let the regular horses have their head once in a while so you can live a little."

However, by now we know that the unicorn is real and that we can trust it and ride it, bridle-less, and that it will take us to the right destination and give us joy all along the way. We long to meet its Owner. We even get the idea that if we could take along the other two horses that, with the Owner's help, we could turn them into unicorns too.

A REVIEW OF THE PRINCIPLES AND PRACTICES OF THE SPIRITUAL DIET

As we review the basic principles and practices of the Spiritual diet that have been covered, it will be helpful to think back to the principles and practices of the Physical and the Mental diets. Flip back to chapters 10 and 20 for a moment. By glancing through them first, you will be able to see both how similar and yet how different the Spiritual diet is. (We may also want to recommit ourselves to the Physical and Mental diets that some of us have been slipping on a bit! (Yes, I admit it. I slip too!) Take a look back at pages 43-45 for the Physical diet principles and practices, and at pages 93-95 for the Mental diet overview.

In both the Physical and the Mental lists, the "Practices" do not have to become tasks, or things to check off on our lists, or added burdens in our lives. Rather, they can simply become good habits– things we get used to doing, and thus do naturally and easily.

As you review those principles and practices, notice how the Physical and the Mental match up item for item. Physical food and our physical bodies and this physical earth truly are metaphors or types for all other appetites. Learning to control how we eat and how we enjoy the physical is the perfect school for learning how to use our minds and how to bridle all of our appetites and make them work for our joy and our exaltation rather than toward our destruction.

The Spiritual diet, however, is very different. It is about feasting rather than fasting and about trusting rather than bridling.

The Physical and Mental horses (appetites) of mortality, beautiful and empowering though they can be, will, if unbridled, carry us away from God and kill us both physically and spiritually. But the Spiritual horse is of a different breed which, when trusted and honored, will always take us Home. Our spiritual appetites are to know God, to serve God, to be more like God, to draw near to God, to love God, and to return to God.

The Spiritual horse does not take the initiative as the Physical and Mental horses do. It waits for us to call it and coax it, to use our agency and our gift of choice to make our own decision to mount up and ride. Consequently, the principles and practices we must understand for the spiritual diet are rather different from those we've learned for the physical and mental diets:

Simple Principles of the Spiritual Diet

1. The earth in all its variety and everything in it—all of our mortality—is a great gift from God.

2. The body and brain are godlike additions to the spirit, given here in mortality for the first time in eternity. And the spirit with the body forms the soul of man.

3. Still, the real you is and will always be the spiritual you, the eternal spiritual child of God, now given the gifts of a physical body and mind in order that you might become more like God.

4. With these mortal gifts comes agency, the choice of whether to use mortality or allow mortality to use you.

5. Your spirit has, at its disposal, your body and your brain, which can become its extensions and its tools.

6. Beyond that, the ultimate tool, which can extend our awareness eternally, is the Spirit of the Lord.

7. Spiritual appetites are for prayer, scripture, service, inspiration,

and the Holy Ghost. They all lead us to want to be closer to and more like God.

8. When they are cultivated and magnified, spiritual appetites supersede and exert control over mental and physical appetites. This "shift of horses" is even better than a bridle. Making that choice is the selection of His will over your will, and it acknowledges that He, not you, is the captain of your soul.

9. Spiritual appetites turn us outward rather than inward. They prompt empathy and service.

10. Spiritual appetites are as different from Physical and Mental appetites as the loaves and fishes of the Lord were different from ordinary food. They increase as they are consumed, and they give us an abundance mentality.

11. Slowing down the physical and the mental can speed up the spiritual.

12. Our mortal challenge is to control and bridle the appetites of body and mind and to cultivate and magnify the appetites of the spirit.

13. The spirit, like the body, needs constant nourishment and hydration, and if we wait until we are extremely thirsty before drinking living water, we will experience, without really even being aware of it, chronic spiritual dehydration. Cultivated, encouraged, and prayed for, the thirst for living water can become more powerful than physical thirst.

14. Spiritual feasting is done by receiving the gifts of the Spirit as we feel and express gratitude and appreciation. The expression of gratitude and appreciation to God expands both our awareness and our joy.

15. As we learn to recognize and welcome spiritual appetites, we can feast on both the word and the will of God.

16. Unlike physical things, our possession of spiritual things increases as we give them away.

17. The spiritual perspective is always beautiful and always poetic.

Simple Practices of the Spiritual Diet

1. Do not eat any physical (i.e., toast or orange juice) or mental food (i.e., the newspaper or the news) each day until you have had some spiritual food. (i.e., the scriptures and prayer).

2. Pray "morning, noon, and night." Take "prayer notes," and keep an "ask journal." Pray slowly; read scriptures slowly. Sip and savor the word and the communication of God. Be a good receiver and thus gain discernment and spiritual perspective. Focus the first part of your intake of spiritual food on receiving what is given with joy and gratitude and praise. Listen at least as much as you talk while in prayer. Opt consciously for His will, and mean it. Once a week, have a ten-minute prayer consisting only of thanksgiving, gratitude and praise. On fast Sunday extend the prayer to 20 minutes and thus combine fasting and feasting.

3. Cultivate inspiration by asking for and then acting on spiritual nudges or impressions each day.

4. Sing a song from the hymnbook early each morning (with self or family) and then read the two scriptures that go with it.

5. Carry scripture with you. Consider carrying a different standard work each season.

6. Strive to see people's spirit rather than their body. (Ask for "Namaste.")

7. Use an hour of the Sabbath day to spiritually create the week ahead.

Different horse, different principles, different practices–but these are the ones that convert diet into discipleship!

THIRD INTERMISSION

DIET REDEFINED

Now, set aside the horses-as-appetites metaphor for a moment (we will come back to it) and simply think of yourself as your eternal spirit, which now inhabits a mortal form. You, (your spirit you) has a couple of fantastic tools at its disposal–your brain and your body. You (your spirit) can use your brain/body tool in so many ways. The mind has vastly more power and potential than we generally use. You can program it to seek out and recognize whatever you want it to. You can use it in small ways (like an alarm clock–I can take a nap and tell my brain to wake me in exactly 30 minutes, or 45, or 10, and it never misses by more than a few seconds) or in large ways like programming it to warn you of danger or to wonder at beauty or to develop an embryonic idea within its subconscious. You can also program your body to be more responsive to stimulus or to ward off infection or to heighten or sharpen its senses.

Besides the powerful (and vastly underused) tools of brain and body, we also have access to ultimate power, awareness and perspective because of our capacity to plug in to the Spirit–the Holy Ghost–the actual third personage of the Godhead. (Think of the brain as a powerful but limited laptop [or "headtop"] computer that can connect to the limitless "mainframe" of the Spirit.) While we can't program the Holy Ghost, we can access His enormous power and perspective and hook up wirelessly to whatever insights and inspirations we truly need.

Think of that: The vastly powerful and underused tool of mind and brain, given, for the first time during this mortality, is completely programmable by the real you (your eternal spirit). And the ultimate awareness, perspective and illumination source and guidance system of the Holy Ghost is always available for connection.

There are two basic ways to approach a day. One is to get up, make a list, plan the day, and go out and try to check everything off, being always proactive and in control. On the surface, this sounds pretty good–and it certainly is what most people either try to do or think they should be doing.

The alternative is to get up and Program and Pray. First, program your mind by essentially telling it that you want it to use its full capacity to give you awareness and perspective as the day unfolds. Instruct your brain to seek and find awareness of beauty, of taste, of people and their needs and feelings, of ideas and connections, of new ways to see and do things, and most of all, of God's will and of what He wants you to see, and think, and do. Give your brain the programming command to sip and savor life and the good and important things in it. And program your mind to gather and discover perspective of how things look to others, how seeming coincidences fit together, how opportunities could be developed and problems solved, and how God views things and responds to people.

Second, pray for the Spirit to take you beyond even the expanded capacities of your mind and to give to you additional awareness and perspective of all these things–and to give you the impressions, nudges, and guidance that will allow you to do what He wants you to do that day rather than what you want–what He knows is best rather than what you think is best.

I believe that the desire for and effort to force the day and its circumstances to go as we want leads to frustration and often to false paths, because it is based on the false premise that we control things and that we know what is best for us and those around us.

Those who try, day in and day out, to take the first approach end up finding themselves "kicking against the pricks" as the scripture says–constantly trying to force things to go the way they planned them, including other people and situations (and even time itself). But things never quite go as planned or conform to what they had envisioned.

The real problem with this approach (beyond the frustration) is that you miss so much. Trying to use the brain to accomplish and check off the things on your list no matter what, rather than to give you added awareness and perspective, wastes the mind's capacity and puts it to a task it is less suited for. Most importantly, by focusing on your own will, you lose sight of (or never gain sight of) His will.

When we take the Program and Pray alternative, we still have goals, and we still may make a list, and we certainly still plan. The difference is that we do it prayerfully, trying to get as much guidance as we can in advance of the day. And we do it as a "tentative, best effort plan," acknowledging both to God and to ourselves that we know way too little to do a final plan, and that our desire is to do His will and not ours.

This attitude is the perfect preparation for programming the brain and then praying to the Spirit for all we can muster of awareness and perspective, and for the added measure that the Spirit can bring. Then we go forth, tentative plan in hand, with both our own limited brains and the unlimited Spirit working in tandem to reveal to us the beauties, the opportunities, and the Lord's will for the moments that make up the day ahead.

We trust His guidance, we expect it because we have asked for it, and we know that its ultimate source is connected to our soul. The day becomes an adventure and a serendipitous feast.

Now, back to the Three Horses and Two Bridles

Programming the body and the brain, of course, is an advanced way of bridling the Physical and Mental horses. Mortal appetites and passions and senses become trained to open us to greater awareness, perspective, beauty and connections with others. We become part of the horses and work with them even as we master and bridle them. They extend and enhance us and bring us to joy. Praying for the guidance of the Spirit and for the impressions and nudges and guidance that give us His gifts and lead us to His will is an advanced way of riding the Unicorn and letting it take us home.

"Diet," in this context, means so much more than our conventional definition. It is the sequential training of two horses and the subsequent discovery of a third horse that is so much more, and that trains us and takes us to a new home.

The marvelous bridling metaphor of James and Alma becomes the framework (and the key to understanding) three levels of truth: physical, mental/emotional, and spiritual. Appetites, passions, and desires are transformed from our obsessions and potential addictions to become first our servants, then our friends, and finally our spiritual prompters. Within this paradigm, life becomes joyous, and the Gospel becomes more exciting, more positive, and more meaningful. Through Alma and James's lens, we can now connect this redefined diet or paradigm to every aspect of the Gospel, and to virtually every aspect of life. The final ten chapters, which I call Supplements and Afterthoughts, do some of this connecting.

SUPPLEMENTS

AND

AFTERTHOUGHTS

CONNECTING AND COMBINING
THE BRIDELL DIET WITH THE
WORD OF WISDOM

The most powerful and correct physical diet ever known came as revelation from God. The Word of Wisdom is God's own revelation, through a Prophet, on physical health. Hopefully no principle or practice of my Bridell eat-half diet is at variance with the Lord's advice and standard. Let me go further than that; hopefully every principle and practice I have advocated is in harmony and complementary to "the Word."

The Bridell diet is about portions and pace and bridling appetites so that they give us joy. It rests on the premise that our bodies, if disciplined to limited quantity, will become more discerning and more demanding of quality. Thus it does not get into what to eat and what not to eat. One reason I felt no need to do that is that it has already been done by God himself in the 89th Section of the Doctrine and Covenants. I invite you to add the "what" of the Word of Wisdom to the "how" of the eat-half diet.

Perhaps the simplest and most direct way to compare, harmonize and complement is to go phrase by phrase from the revelation: The following words and word groups (in italics) are directly from the scripture, and they are in sequence:

Word of Wisdom (D&C 89:1)

The word "wisdom" implies restraint, and controlled pace, and awareness . . . suggesting slowness and peace.

For the benefit (v. 1)

A good diet is for the benefit of the user. A proactive diet, where bridling and control gain the upper hand is a positive thing. It is not a restriction or a penalty or a bitter pill, but a benefit and a joy–a natural and normal thing to do where we follow both the needs and the controlled desires of our mortal bodies.

To be sent greeting (v. 2)

The Lord gives us His wisdom about eating as a greeting and as a joy first of all. It is also a warning, which He mentions later. But it opens cordially, as a greeting, as an invitation to make the best of and maximize the joy of the mortal earth and body which He has given us–gifts so great that when we first heard of them in the premortal life, we "shouted for joy."

Not by . . . constraint (v. 2)

Laws of health and counsel about how to maximize our joy and fully use and appreciate our bodies are not to constrain us but to set us free–free from the impediments and limitations that can come upon us when we fail to use wisdom in caring for our bodies. When appetite is bridled, it becomes our friend and we can trust it and use it to enhance our joy.

By revelation (v. 2)

This is not a set of Joseph Smith's ideas or impressions. It is from the Father of our spirits and the creator of our bodies. It is direct from Him, and is called revelation.

The order and will of God (v. 2)

It is what He wants for us, because He wants us to have all He has–and His body is perfect. There is a cause-and-effect order in His world and in His universe. He knows all of the laws and gives them to us for our benefit. If we live within His order and seek His will, we will reap the physical and spiritual blessings He offers us. It is not God's will for our appetites to control us; it is His will for us to control our appetites.

Temporal salvation (v. 2)

This term at first sounds a bit like an oxymoron. Salvation is eternal isn't it, not temporal? Or is it both? We know that this temporal earth and our temporal bodies ("telestial" is another name for both of them) can evolve to a celestial level as they are saved and exalted. We must worry about and care for our bodies not only so they will function well and serve us joyously while here, but also so they can become the perfected bodies that will be a part of our eternal souls. The Physical and Mental horses can't become perfected until they blend and become one with the Spiritual horse.

All saints in the last days (v. 2)

These truths and diet laws apply to all. And we do live in the last days–in a time more filled with stress and conflict and opposite extremes than any time before. The strain and demands of these times are greater than ever before, and require the health and durability that will get us through them. Never before have bridles been so needed and so important.

A principle with promise (v. 3)

This is my favorite line because the Word of Wisdom is a series of true principles defined as the reality that God has put in place with consistent, predictable results. Correct principles ring true in our souls; they always produce rewards and positive results when adhered to–and penalties and punishments when ignored or violated. Because they are clear and consistent principles, they carry promises of reliable results. Their rewards are not capricious or random; they are promised and guaranteed. The Lord knows how our bodies work because He created them. He knows that if we bridle the appetites and passions within them by following true principles, they will work for our good and enable us to return to Him and be more like Him. The principles must be simple, and must be implementable by way of the simple practices that become good habits.

Adapted to the capacity of the weak (v. 3)

A diet should not be laborious or unnatural. It should be logical and rational and even beautiful. And it should be accessible to all, requiring no special or extraordinary strength to implement it. Rather, it should require understanding, commitment, and faith, all of which are enhanced by our own humility and admission of weakness.

In consequence of evils and designs in the hearts of conspiring men (v. 4)

Appetites are fed by self-serving designs and profit-motive conspiracies. Advertisers use appetites (along with their own slick deceptions) to make us think we need what we really only want. Many forces combine to make our Physical horse want to run away with us, but it is only we, ourselves, that can use the bridle.

I have warned you and forewarn you (v. 4)

Although opening as a greeting, the scripture is also a warning–first of all about things that should not be taken into our bodies at all, in any quantity. These are not things to use in moderation, but things to avoid altogether. Not things to eat half of, but to eat none of.

Wine or strong drink . . . is not good (v. 5)

Not any time, or any where, or for any occasion.

Strong drinks are not for the belly (v. 7)

Never, not at all.

Tobacco is not for the body . . . and is not good for man (v. 8)
Simply and totally avoid its use.

Hot drinks are not for the body (v. 9)
The reference was clearly to coffee and tea, and again, this is avoidance, not moderation.

We will continue with the "second half" of the Word of Wisdom in the next chapter. Most of the second half, as you know, is about what to eat–the positive side of the equation which ties most closely to the proactive and grateful tone that the Bridell diet tries to emphasize.

WORD OF WISDOM
CONNECTIONS II

The simplest and most direct way to compare, harmonize and complement the Bridell diet with the Word of Wisdom is to go phrase by phrase from the revelation. Chapter 30 reviewed the phrases from the "explanatory and regulatory" first half of the 89th Section. This chapter picks up where we left off and covers the "positive, promising" second half of the revelation. The following word groups in italics are directly from the scripture.

All wholesome herbs God hath ordained for the
constitution, nature, and use of man (v. 10)
The crux of the Bridell diet is to eat half of three meals and half of a couple of snacks with the one exception being herbs, fruits and vegetables of which can be eaten more liberally.

Every herb in the season thereof, and every fruit in the season (v. 11)
Perhaps the most pivotal promise of the Bridell diet is that, after you cut quantity to one half, realizing that this is all it is going to get, your body will begin to demand better quality. When this happens,

fruit, vegetables, grains, and other things mentioned in the Word of Wisdom become more and more appealing. Fruits and vegetables are best (in both taste and nourishment) when we consume them in their natural season, fresh from the plant.

To be used with prudence and thanksgiving (v. 11)

Another "key to Bridell" is to eat slowly (or with prudence), in small bites, sipping and smelling and savoring, and enjoying and being grateful for each morsel. All eating thus becomes a little celebration of God's goodness and of the marvels of the physical earth and the physical body—a mini-Thanksgiving, if you will.

Flesh also of beasts and of fowls I have ordained for the use of man. nevertheless they are to be used sparingly (v. 12)

Meat is one of the wonderful foods that requires particular regulation and moderation. Used sparingly it rounds out our diet and gives strength. Unregulated it not only causes physical problems but also pulls our appetite away from the fruit of the fields which get left out and neglected.

. . . Only in times of winter, or of cold, or famine (v. 13)

Once "tuned" by appetite control, our bodies desire and crave at least modest portions of meat in colder weather, and may want none at all in warmer months.

All grain is ordained for the use of man (v. 14)

Because of its "carbs," bread is excluded from many of today's fad diets. However, used in moderation (or in "half" in Bridell terminology) whole grains truly are . . .

To be the staff of life (v. 14)

Indeed!

Also the fruit of the vine (v. 16)

As we become consistent in eating half, our bodies become much more selective in what they hunger for, and one of the main things they want is fresh fruit, "vine ripened," if you will.

Fruit, whether in the ground or above the ground (v. 16)

We can enjoy all kinds of fruit and vegetables, and what a marvelous variety we have today. Each one is unique and a gift from God. I was at a dinner party the other night where the host had made a special tomato salad containing seven different kinds of tomatoes, each fresh, and each with its own particular flavor—each to be sipped and savored.

Wheat for man (v. 17)

Whole wheat that is, full of so much that we need. And have you noticed that, when you are "half hungry" because of the established practice of eating half, that piece of good whole-grain bread is a marvel of taste and texture and simply feels like it was made for us to enjoy and benefit from.

Barley for mild drinks (v. 17)

Pero or Postum drinks are made from barley; nothing better on a cold winter morning.

All saints who remember to keep and do these sayings (v. 18)

Here come the promises for simply following commandments and the admonition to bridle our appetite for food.

Shall receive health in their navel (v. 18)

The navel connects to organs, to digestion, to blood supply. This refers to health in the areas that need to be open and free of obstructions and that carry oxygen and nourishment to every cell of our bodies.

And marrow to their bones (v. 18)

In the marrow lies our immune systems. This is a promise of wellness and of relative freedom from disease.

And shall find wisdom (v. 19)

The blessings of physical bridling are mental and spiritual. And this one is so great that the whole revelation was named after it.

And great treasures of knowledge (v. 19)

Again the rewards start with a healthier and trimmer physical body, but the greatest benefits transcend the physical and flow into our minds and souls.

Even hidden treasures (v. 19)

Some of these mental and spiritual treasures would never even be seen or imagined without the Holy Ghost, who reveals so much to our spirits when we are receptive. However, these treasures are hidden from those whose spirits are not receptive.

And shall run and not be weary (v. 20)

A well-bridled horse conserves and magnifies its strength.

And shall walk and not faint (v. 20)

Endurance starts with the physical but extends to "enduring to the end" and thus returning to God.

A promise, that the destroying angel shall pass by them (v. 21)

We escape, among other things, the destructive, dark angel of gluttony.

The Bridell diet supports and conforms to the Word of Wisdom, not the other way around. The eat-half diet is a methodology designed to help us implement and fully benefit from The Lord's own law of health

CHAPTER

MORE SPIRITUAL
CONNECTIONS

Besides Section 89, another section in the Doctrine and Covenants is extremely relevant to the Bridell diet: Section 59. It is so powerful and so relevant that it prompts thought not only about its connections to the diet but also about another principle and practice that should be included as part of the diet. First though, let's go through the relevant phrases of the section just as we did with Section 89

Go to the house of prayer and offer up thy sacraments upon my holy day (v. 9)

There is a connection between observance of the Sabbath day, the good food of the earth, and the health and strength of the physical body. When we attend church and partake of the sacrament, we are not only worshiping but also making a connection that benefits us physically and spiritually.

This is a day appointed unto you to rest from your labors (v. 10)

Although not much was said in the Bridell diet about rest, much was implied. The slower pace of eating, the awareness of sipping and

163

savoring, and the poetic approach to life are all part of rest, and they all slow down our body and our spirit to allow more inspiration and to promote more peace, serenity, and rejuvenation.

And to pay thy devotions unto the Most High (v. 10)

Sunday is indeed the best day for slower, more thoughtful prayer, devotion, and re-commitment. The Lord made the Sabbath for man and not man for the Sabbath–and He deems it so important that it is among His Ten Commandments. This marvelous 59th section gives us the spirit and the specific promises behind that importance.

Let thy food be prepared with singleness of heart (v. 13)

Again, that slow, deliberate, grateful attitude that is part of the diet is also part of the Sabbath and of fasting.

That thy fasting may be perfect, or, in other words,
that thy joy may be full (v. 13)

Remarkably, "fasting" is a synonym for "joy." Fasting, in this context, implies appreciation, gratitude, awareness and a spiritual context–which are the hallmarks of the Bridell diet.

This is fasting and prayer, or in other words,
rejoicing and prayer (v. 14)

Again, rejoicing is a synonym for fasting or for the denial and self-control involved in what we eat (or do not eat). And it goes together with prayer, with worship, and with thanks.

Do these things with thanksgiving, with cheerful hearts
and countenances (v. 15)

So the challenge is the bridling, controlling and mastering of all your physical appetites, and the appreciation and proper use of all of your God-given passions. Such mastery cheers and gladdens your heart and gives you the promise of the next verse.

Inasmuch as ye do this, the fullness of the earth is yours (v. 16)

What a promise! We control our appetite, we fast with joy, and the whole earth and all of mortality works together for our happiness.

The herb and the good things which come
of the earth. . . for food (v. 17)

The earth, like our bodies, is mortal but can become immortal. The connection between body and earth is a connection of joy, and when the spirit is in control, our bodies will crave the good things of the earth. When our spirits control the quantity, our bodies will begin to desire more quality, and we will discern the truly good things of the earth and no longer want too much.

All things which come of the earth, in the season thereof, are made
for the benefit and the use of man (v. 18)

All the natural things of the earth, when they are fresh, are to be used, enjoyed, and savored.

Both to please the eye and to gladden the heart (v. 18)

Partaking of them in a measured, controlled, appreciative way, is both an artistic and a joyful experience that can repeat itself many times each day.

It pleaseth God that he hath given all these things to man (v. 20)

What a lovely thought, that it brings joy to God as well as to us.

For unto this end were they made to be used,
with judgment, not to excess (v. 20)

"Used" is the operative word. We should use the things of the earth, not let them use us. Appetites and all that they lead us to are wonderful, an integral part of God's plan, as long as we use them correctly, with judgment, and not to excess. A good rider shows the horse who is boss, and then comes the joy of real riding. By the same token, a person who lives life to its fullest will show his appetites who is boss–then comes the joy of real living.

Now, think of the implications! Frankly, this section forces us to add at least one more principle and practice to the Bridell diet! Let's build the next chapter around it.

THE IMPORTANCE OF
THE SABBATH DAY
IN THE BRIDELL DIET

Everything that has been presented in this diet has come, directly or indirectly, from scripture. I believe that is why it rings true and why we can think of it on so many different levels. I have come to believe more strongly than ever that everything on this earth is a "type and a shadow" of spiritual and eternal truths, and that one of the strongest and most useful metaphors of all is food/eating/drinking/hungering/thirsting.

As I wrote the last chapter, the 59th Section seemed to beg for even more discussion, because the Sabbath day is an indispensable part of any true law of health and any complete diet.

The Sabbath is the Lord's renewal and calibration tool. It can reset our bodies as well as our souls. It can provide the reassessment that keeps us on course to progress that is regular, measurable, and consistent. It adds new meaning to the truth that "The Sabbath was made for man, and not man for the Sabbath" (Mark 2:27).

God gave us this day, and this concept of a seventh day to bless us. He made us in such a way that we function best when we "shut down and reset" each seven days. He made the earth this way too, so that when land is given a "sabbatical" and allowed to lie fallow and rest each seventh year it becomes more productive and more vital. Many of the gifts promised for Sabbath observance relate to the earth, and that "the fullness" of it will be ours if we observe the Sabbath.

The key ingredient of a well-observed Sabbath is worship, which we usually think of as a spiritual and mental process. But it can also be partially physical. We can worship with our bodies by fasting and by purging and purifying them. Fast Sundays are the prime time to do this, but every Sunday can be a partial fast as we eat less, eat slower, eat purer and better. Putting the body at rest can activate and energize and give focus to the spirit.

A good summary of what we should try to do on the Sabbath can be made up of "re" words: rest, rejuvenate, renew, reset, re-create, review, recalibrate, and replenish.

Some of us use Sunday dinner as a time to feast, even to gorge. Let me suggest doing the opposite. Simplify your food on Sundays. Eat very slowly, and eat only the best and most healthy food. Prepare food simply and with singleness of heart. Eat little or nothing before attending church and partaking of the Sacrament.

Let me further suggest some specific weekly reassessments that I believe can become a powerful part of one's physical worship on Sundays:

1. Keep a Sunday journal where you write the feelings and impressions you have during your worship and prayer.
2. As part of your entry each week, record three things relating to your diet:

    - Your weight
    - How you have felt physically during the past week, and
    - What foods and types of foods appeal to you most

    Don't expect dramatic change week by week, but keep track of the steady progress of the eat-half diet.

3. Visualize. Sit back for a few moments and close your eyes and try to see in your mind both an external and an internal view of your improving physical self:

   The external view: Don't be extreme or wildly unrealistic. Don't try to see yourself 50 pounds lighter or perfect in every way, but visualize improvement. See yourself trimmer, healthier, getting stronger. Visualize yourself moving better, eating slower, becoming firmer and straighter and more energized.

   The internal view: Think about the systems within your body and try to see them in your mind's eye. Your digestive system, clear and functional, not weighted down or bloated or at over-capacity, but smooth and efficient. Visualize your circulatory system open and flowing, your breathing open and easy, your blood oxygenating. Scriptural phrases can create good visualizing images. "Health in the navel" can prompt positive images of open, flowing and functioning blood vessels and organs. "Marrow in the bones" can help visualize strong immune systems and bones, and so on.

Let Sundays be your day of reassessment—spiritually, mentally, and physically. Try to progress from Sunday to Sunday. Have modest but motivating weekly goals. Ask for help. Become who you know the Lord wants you to be in tiny steps, a week at a time.

CHAPTER

THE ACID TEST: APPLYING
BRIDELL TO HOLIDAY EATING

For so many people, holidays and vacations have become the time for state-of-the-art overeating. Yet, ironically, celebrations, feasts, and holidays can actually be the best times to implement this diet.

The Bridell diet is really, at its core, about enjoying food more, so what better times could there be to employ it than at special, celebratory times of year.

The real trick is to change our assumptions. The old assumption is that the more we eat the more we enjoy, but we know that isn't really true. There is no correlation between the quantity of food we eat and the quantity of joy we feel. In fact, there is usually an inverse relationship. The more we eat, the less joy we find.

The Bridell diet is not about what we shouldn't eat. It is about controlling quantity in a way that allows us to focus more on quality and on the joy of every (small) bite. It's not about what we shouldn't do, but about what we should do to maximize both the joy of eating and the joy of our bodies–and ultimately the joy of our lives. And joy is all about quality and higher consciousness and greater awareness and perspective. It is, in other words (and using the food metaphor), all about sipping and savoring.

Holidays are simply the perfect time to employ the basic Bridell principle of eating half as much twice as slowly. For those who are into the diet and who have begun to reap its rewards, the wonderful and plentiful food of vacations and celebrations will be seen through a different lens; the healthy things will look good to you, and the unhealthy ones will look bad.

Remember that one of the key underlying principles of the diet is that when you cut your quantity to half and hold it at half for many consecutive days, your body, failing to get the greater quantity, will start asking you for greater quality. The main job of your appetite is to get the nutrients into your body that it requires to function, and if your appetite can get you to eat enough junk to get the necessary nutrients, it will do so. But if you enforce the eat-half discipline for long enough, your appetite will realize that the only way to get its nutrients from half the quantity is to demand more quality. You will start craving fruits and vegetables and other wholesome and healthy foods and will gradually start loathing the greasy, heavy, or refined junk foods. You want this to begin happening before big holidays, especially Thanksgiving and Christmas; so start now, recommit, and have your appetites in training before the next holiday hits.

Let's do a quick review of the Physical diet, thinking of holidays or feasts or big family dinners and the "eating temptations" they hold. As you read through the principles, think how well they apply (and how important they are) at a time when there is so much focus on eating.

Then, as you read through the practices, try to visualize yourself living by them at parties, at dinners, and even just walking around your festive house. Visualize yourself walking past food and not picking it up unless it is mealtime or snack-time (three half meals, two half snacks, nothing else).

Visualize yourself drinking a tall glass of water before each meal or snack. Visualize yourself eating what you want at those meals and snacks, but only half of it. Visualize yourself eating very slowly, with small bites, smelling and savoring the food, and sipping whatever you drink. Visualize yourself eating the quality food that lends itself to small bites and savoring.

Visualize yourself writing a simple, private poem about the tastes and smells of an anticipated holiday or vacation. Visualize yourself finding time to slip away for a walk or a jog or whatever your chosen form of exercise is. Visualize a lovely celebration and family time, full of flavor, of awareness, of perspective, and of the kind of bridling that fills you with love!

PROOF FROM RHODE ISLAND

Proof shows up in the strangest places—such as in USA Today. A recent issue featured an article by Nanci Hellmich titled "Study Suggests Eating Slowly Translates into Eating Less." In the study, a group of women were invited to eat lunch in a laboratory on two separate occasions. The first time they were told to eat as quickly as they could; the second lunch they were instructed to eat slowly and put down their forks between bites. Both times they were instructed to stop eating when they were comfortably full. The article reports that the women consumed 646 calories in about nine minutes in the "quick-eating" test, but averaged 579 calories in about 29 minutes in the "slow-eating" test.

"They ate 67 more calories in nine minutes than they did in 29 minutes," said lead researcher Kathleen Melanson, director of the Rhode Island University Energy Metabolism. She summarized the importance of the findings: "If you add that up over three meals a day, that's a big difference . . . One way to help control calorie intake is to slow down and savor and enjoy your food more."[8]

When the women were eating more slowly they predictably drank more water, and just as predictably said they enjoyed the meal more than when they were hurrying. An hour afterward, the women were less satisfied and hungrier when they had eaten quickly compared with then they had eaten slowly.

So, there you go. It seems that the Bridell diet has now been validated by a university energy metabolism laboratory. But none of us needed that verification, did we? Because the real proof lies in doing it ourselves. We feel better, we look better, and we end up eating better food, and enjoying it more. More importantly, we learn and apply spiritual principles of awareness and perspective in the process!

WHO IS WINNING?

I have been traveling a lot lately and watching people eat wherever I go. It is so interesting to sit in a restaurant or an airport or a fast food place and watch people eat. I always watch to see who is winning–the person or the appetite. Usually the appetite is winning.

When the appetite is winning, people eat fast. Their fork is loading up the next bite the second they get the previous bite in their mouth. Their eyes are darting around from plate to fork and over to the bread and then to their drink, like they are protecting their food as they gulp and guzzle it down.

Even in very nice restaurants, you see a lot of appetites winning. The bites are big and too rapid in their succession. It's a subconscious thing; the person may be carrying on a conversation and using good table manners, but if you look closely, the appetite is winning.

It's so refreshing when you see someone who is winning over the appetite, who is bridling, who is reining in the horse and thus enjoying it more. I like to watch someone taking his or her time, smelling and savoring the food, arranging a small bite on the fork, then setting the fork down between bites and chewing slowly. These people have a much calmer demeanor. There is a look of control and peace and awareness of what is around them as well as what is on their plate, and these people never seem to be seriously overweight.

We need to learn to ask ourselves as we are eating, "Who is the master here, and who is the servant? Who is winning, me or my appetite?"

Although our fast food re-fueling places are taking over the world, spreading one of the worst images of America, Europeans generally do a better job with small bites and with sipping and savoring than Americans. In most cities in Europe, it is much easier to find people really enjoying their food and taking their time, finding that little bit of joy in each small, well-composed bite.

The cool thing is that you don't need a fancy restaurant and fine china and silver in order to eat in a refined (and diet conscious) way. It's all in the head. I saw a fellow sitting on a New York park bench in the sun on an unseasonably warm winter day, head back, taking in the rays, and eating, very slowly and thoughtfully, a sauerkraut hot dog on a Kaiser roll; he was the master, his appetite the servant.

I've been thinking about the phrase "healthy appetite." Perhaps we need to re-define what that means. Sometimes we picture it as a really hungry person, wolfing down his food. Actually, that is an unhealthy appetite—an appetite that is winning, and that is doing damage to the body doing the eating.

A better definition of a healthy appetite is a controlled appetite, a bridled appetite that goes only as fast and only as far as the rider wants it to go and that enjoys every step or every bite. That kind of appetite is truly healthy, both physically and spiritually, and will serve us well for both the short term and the long.

Watch people eat and see what you think. And then watch yourself eat. Make it a beautiful thing. Over time, it will make you a beautiful thing too.

THE POWER OF NAPPING

Yes, yes, I know that diet books are supposed to be about eating and not about sleeping. But as you well know by now, this diet is about much more than food. It is about maximizing our time here on earth–physically, mentally and spiritually. And guess what? Sleeping is a big part of our time here and deserves some mention.

Did you know that people who take a semi-regular brief nap in the afternoon or early evening have a 37% lower incident of heart attacks? Here are some excerpts (with my commentary) from a *Newsweek* article.

"Researchers at the Harvard School of Public Health and the University of Athens Medical School have just released findings from a large study that shows how midday napping reduces one's chance of coronary mortality by more than a third. So go ahead and nap–a short daily snooze might ward off a heart attack later in life."[9]

The study looked at 23,681 individuals living in Greece who had no history of coronary heart disease, stroke or cancer when they first volunteered. What they found was pretty amazing. More than six years later, those who napped at least three times per week for an average of at least 30 minutes had a 37 percent lower coronary mortality than those who took no naps.

This is no surprise to countries traditionally fond of siestas (regions such as southern Italy, southern Greece, and several Latin American countries, all of which have low mortality rates from heart disease).

And it's not just the Harvard and Medical Archives studies that show the benefits of napping. NASA sleep researchers discovered that "a nap of 26 minutes can boost performance by as much as 34 percent." And a Stanford University School of Medicine study (2006) showed that "napping resulted in improved mood, increased alertness and reduced lapses in performance among doctors and nurses."[10]

How about that?

Now you may be saying, "Wait a minute. I would love to take a nap every day, but who are these people? Don't they have kids? Don't they have jobs? How do you just take a nap in the afternoon?" Hold off on those practical questions for a minute. I will get to them at the end of the column. Let's stay theoretical for a minute or two longer and look at some other benefits of naps.

Studies indicate that 20 minutes of sleep in the afternoon provides more rest than 20 minutes more sleep in the morning (though the last two hours of morning sleep have special benefits of their own). The body seems to be designed for this, as most people's bodies naturally become more tired in the afternoon, about eight hours after we wake up.

Many experts advise to keep the nap between 15 and 30 minutes, as sleeping longer gets you into deeper stages of sleep from which it's more difficult to awaken.

Although John F. Kennedy, Winston Churchill, Albert Einstein, Thomas Edison, Johannes Brahms, Napoleon Bonaparte, Leonardo da Vinci and a long list of other historic figures reportedly loved to catnap, many Americans still associate napping with people who are lazy, stupid or don't have the right stuff.

Napping at work is not the norm. A stigma is attached to it. It's OK for people to go out to exercise at noontime but not to nap.

Many people feel a mid-afternoon slump in mood and alertness is caused by a poor night of sleep or eating a heavy lunch. However, in reality, this occurs because we were meant to have a mid-afternoon nap.

Several lines of evidence, including the universal tendency of toddlers and the elderly to nap in the afternoon and the afternoon nap of siesta cultures, have led sleep researchers to the same conclusion: nature intended that we take a nap in the middle of the day. This biological readiness to fall asleep in the mid-afternoon coincides with a slight drop in body temperature and occurs regardless of whether or not we eat lunch. It is present even in good sleepers who are well rested.

So, there are lots of well-documented evidences of the benefits of a little nap in the afternoon, but it is disregarded by most of us because of two rather overpowering feelings:

1. I am too busy or too occupied (by work or by kids) to nap.
2. I can't just lie down and go to sleep. My body doesn't work that way.

Many people say "Yes, yes, I understand that naps are good, but I just can't lie down and fall asleep. My mind won't turn off that easily. I would just be lying there and thinking about the things I should be doing, and the whole thing would be frustrating. I would feel like I was wasting time."

Well, OK, but listen for a minute. You know me pretty well by now, and you know that Dr. Bridell is not too easily persuaded by excuses. Remember, I happen to think that the body–and the whole physical world–is a metaphor for the spiritual, and that how we take care of our bodies is going to largely determine (and be the model for) how we take care of our spirits.

Eating and sleeping (and how we do both of them) are two of the four most important things we do for our bodies (the other two are exercise and breathing, which we have talked about in earlier chapters.) So let me attempt to persuade you that you may not want to dismiss this napping idea too quickly.

Lots of moms, busy and overwhelmed as they are, find opportunities for a little nap. Moms with young children may find a few minutes while their kids are napping. Moms with school kids may find a brief opportunity before the school kids come home. People at work may find a place where they can lie down for a few moments, or even rest their head on the desk like we used to do in the school library.

Here is the key: Napping, like eating slowly and eating half, is a skill you can learn and a taste you can acquire! The first few times you try it, you may not get to sleep, or if you do, you may wake up groggy, or disoriented, or wake up too late or too tired so you wish you hadn't tried it. But you can learn how to nap in a way that is beneficial.

You can actually program your mind to wake you up in 10 minutes, or 20, or whatever you have. You can look at the dial of your watch and say "the minute hand is on the three right now, and I will wake up when it is on the six." You can learn to turn off your mind and go mentally blank and drift quickly into sleep. You can think of a little nap as the re-set button that re-syncs your brain and your energy. You can do all this with a little practice.

Don't make napping a chore, and don't feel you have to schedule it every day. Try to find the right moment two or three times a week and let it grow on you. If you don't get to sleep in your designated little time, don't worry. Rest is almost as good, and maybe you will drift off next time. Just get as comfortable as you can and try to completely relax.

Some find that they have to relax their body one part at a time, first concentrating on relaxing their neck muscles, then their hands and feet, then their legs and arms, etc. Try different things. Find your own way to turn off your body and your mind for a few minutes, and let the sleep come or not come.

Now here is the personal part, the Dr. Bridell testimonial part, the true confessions by me part. I get my best work done early in the morning and late at night. When people ask me if I am a "lark" (early riser) or an "owl" (stay-up-late type), I say "both" because I think the early morning and the late night are the two best parts of the day. They are the quietest, the most beautiful. They are the times to write and to think which are my two favorite things to do. But people usually consider them mutually exclusive—that you can't have them both.

Well, I wanted them both, and that is what led me to my napping habit. I find that if I can take a little nap in the late afternoon, just when I am running down and getting drowsy because I got up early, I get recharged and feel great for the evening, even the late evening. So there is my own personal thinking (and practice) on the matter.

Different people have different needs, different lifestyles, different ways of living each day. But most people can benefit from learning to take a nap a few afternoons a week.

It's worth fooling around with. It's worth a little experimentation. It's worth the 10 or 20 minutes you find to try it. There is no downside and lots of upside to trying. And it fits extremely well with the Bridell diet. It is another way of training your body and your mind to serve your spirit.

As you get a little better at the art of napping, clearer thought and better ideas will start to come to you, often right after a little nap. Your head will be clearer, and the spirit will speak to you a bit easier. A nap will give you that little re-charge you need to relish rather than resist the rest of the day.

THE ADDICTIONS OF PERSONAL TECHNOLOGY

Play a guessing game with me. What am I thinking of that tastes good; that is "more-ish"; that is comfortable to do, especially when other things aren't going so well; that can be good and hearty, but is often damaging and unhealthy; that can be used as a pleasurable and sustaining asset but that can also take over your life?

It could be food, right? That is the obvious answer, since the food appetite is the type for all other appetites. It could be a lot of things that appeal to our appetites. One thing it could be, and that it is for a lot of us: Technology! The personal and potentially addictive technologies of Internet, ipod, e-mail, video games, cell phones, digital cameras, downloads, blackberrys, voice mail, palm pilots, etc.

Think about the people you know (are any of them you?) who can't sit through lunch without checking their e-mail or their voice mail a couple of times, who only take their headphones off when they have to, who spend more time in virtual reality than in real reality. Think of those who sit down at the Internet and don't get up for hours, who talk on the cell phone while driving, shopping, eating, walking, working, who spend more time entering their to-do list than working on it, who feel anxiety attacks when they are out of wireless range or, heaven forbid, out of range of cell phone coverage.

For many, it is hard to imagine what they did with their time 10 or 15 years ago before personal electronic devices existed. More than half of their time is spent on them now, so what did they do with that half of their time back then? Maybe they read books or did sports or walked or went out in nature, or attended the theater or visited, in person, with other human beings. Imagine that!

The questions we should ask ourselves are so similar to the questions an overeating person has to ask himself. What could you do if you weren't eating (Googling or game playing) all the time? What would you feel like if you were not carrying all that extra weight (extra useless information)? What is all that food (data) doing to you, to your outlook, your brain, your body? Why are the bad foods (bad sites, games, etc) the most addictive of all?

The cures would be similar too: Take smaller portions, eat only at certain times of the day, turn off the technology and ignore it at other times, maybe cut your time-use in half, and see if your brain starts wanting better stuff from technology when you only consume half as much. See if you start wanting more quality as you restrict your quantity.

Is technology bad? Do our personal electronic devices have to take over our lives? Of course not–just as food is not bad and eating does not have to take over our lives. But as with any appetite, there can be a dangerous, even insidious progression from appetite to obsession to addiction.

It is so important to think of technology as a tool, as the means to other desired ends, and not as an end in itself. Just as with food, if we limit our intake by confining our use to certain restricted times of the day it will become necessary to use that limited time more effectively. We will go only to the sites that really help us, make only the calls we need to make, and listen only to the music that really uplifts.

A good way to check yourself (and to check your appetite for technology) is to simply ask yourself, fairly often, "Who's winning? Who is in charge here–me or the technology?" If your cell phone is always on and you feel you have to answer it, or at least see who it is, or check the message immediately, then your cell phone is winning. If you can't walk past your computer without checking e-mail or looking at a couple of your favorite sites, then your computer is in charge. If those white ipod earphone lines are always connected to your ears, you are obsessed. If you spend more time on video games than reading scriptures or attending church, you might be more addicted than you think.

Learn to use the marvels of technology to help you reach conscious goals. Think of electronic devices as tools that can help you to be what you want to be and accomplish what you want to do. But be in charge. Think it through. Use technology according to your rules and priorities, and don't let it pull you into someone else's idea of what is interesting or important.

GIVING CREDIT TO
JAMES AND ALMA–AND
ENDING WITH JOY

While we have referred to the book of James in the New Testament and to Alma's letter to his son Shiblon several times, we have never given these great prophets full credit for the beautiful bridling metaphor.

Although I try hard not to reveal too much personal information about myself, I will tell you that James is my favorite book of scripture. Whether or not he was the Lord's half brother as many experts suggest, he was a powerful and poetic writer who captured the essence of the Gospel in his five brief chapters.

I have repeatedly quoted James 3:3 where he speaks of "bridling the whole body," and says "We put bits in the horses' mouths, that they may obey us; and we turn about their whole body." He is referring specifically to bridling our tongues, and the enormous potential for evil and destruction that small member has.

But I love the broader picture that James paints through his bridle metaphor. The bit, like the tongue, is in the mouth, and the mouth is the part we have to have control over–both in terms of what comes out of it and in terms of what we put into it. The bit is the part of the bridle that allows us to turn the whole body of the horse. The tongue is the part of the body that we have to control if we wish not to hurt others or ourselves with our words. And the mouth, and what goes into it is what we have to learn to bridle if we wish to turn our own whole bodies into the kind of bodies we want them to be.

Bridles, in actuality or in metaphor, are small things that control large things. They are devices that allow us to have control over things that, unbridled, are stronger than we are. Horses, in actuality or in metaphor as an appetite or passion, are large and very powerful things that must be bridled in order to be controlled.

The other scriptural prophet who used the bridle symbolism so well was Alma. I love the letters he wrote to his three sons. The sons were apparently very different from each other, because each of the three letters is completely unique, completely suited to each individual son and his particular needs. The letters reveal Alma as a great parent who understands who each of his sons is and who has thought a lot about exactly what advice each of them needs. I have always been particularly drawn to his letter to Shiblon, in chapter 38. Alma is so proud of this son's "steadiness and faithfulness" and grateful to him for the "great joy he has found in him already" (v. 2).

I think Alma sees in Shiblon a young man of great abilities and strength and passion, so the main thrust of advice is that he control and channel that power, never boasting, being careful of overbearance, and always remembering to give credit to God. Then comes this beautiful, summarizing phrase that I have quoted repeatedly: "see that ye bridle all your passions that ye may be filled with love" (Alma 38:12).

As you have probably guessed because I keep coming back to it, I love this phrase, first because it distinguishes between passion and love. Even more because it teaches us that feelings and passions and appetites grow purer and more beautiful when we learn to control and direct them, and when we apply them correctly and point them in the directions the Lord wants. We grow and expand our love not by letting our passions run away with us, but by mastering them. We get the most joy out of a horse not by letting it run away with us, but by bridling it.

Readers also know by now that I love horses. I rode, just yesterday, up a lovely, early spring canyon, on a horse that took me much further and much faster than I could have gone on my own. I saw more, felt more, and loved more than I could have without that horse, and it was the bridle that kept the joy from turning into danger.

The Bridell Diet is all about bridling and being filled with love. Appetite is not the enemy, but a powerful asset and ally to be used and appreciated and bridled.

Appetite, when bridled, is a source of joy and love. A bridled horse becomes trained and soon starts to take us to where we want to go almost automatically, with only a very light touch from the reins. A trained appetite can start to take us to the right foods in the right quantities almost automatically, without us having to constantly rein it in and hold it back.

The Bridell Diet explains the bridle. As we discipline ourselves to eat half, our appetites gradually change from demanding quantity to demanding quality and begin to take us to where we want to be with very little pressure from our conscious reins. But the initial discipline and training is hard, and we need all the help we can get. You may want to re-read the first ten chapters and be sure you are using all the bridling techniques (water, sipping and savoring, fasting, poetry, etc.) that will be helpful in training your horse.

The most important thing about the whole bridling idea, as James and Alma make so clear, is that it works mentally and spiritually as well as physically. The things that the physical diet can do for your body have counterparts in the things that the mental diet can do for your brain and that the spiritual diet can do for your soul. The bottom line is that the spirit and the body are the soul of man. The physical is a type for the mental and, more importantly for the spiritual. And one of the great gifts of mortality is passions and appetites. For those who learn to bridle them on the physical and mental level, and to ride them freely when they come from the Spirit, life can only get richer and more rewarding (and lighter!) May it all be true for you!

With love, from the mysterious (but really just like you)

Dr. Bridell

ABOUT THE AUTHOR

We (the publisher) asked the mysterious Dr. Bridell if he/she wanted to reveal anything about him/herself in this book, or have any kind of "about the author" page. We received the following note from him/her:

"I actually would like to reveal something about myself–something that I believe is more important than what my real name is or where I live. I would like readers to know how deeply I believe what I have written here and that it has worked (and is working) for me on the physical level (where I have reached and am maintaining the exact weight I have always wanted), on the mental level (where I have a greater clarity and more awareness), and on the spiritual level (where I believe I have started to see the world and my life in it with the perspective God wants me to have).

"The bottom line is that I have become lighter on all three levels! And I think readers deserve to have my own personal testimonial as well as all the others that we printed in the front and back of this book.

"I love using the word 'diet' to describe a philosophy, a lifestyle, and a perspective, and the only thing more fun than writing about it is living it!

"Thanks to all of you who read it and all who try it!"

Dr. Bridell

NOTES

1 From an interview with Guy Claxton in July 2002 conducted by Carl Honore, quoted in Carl Honore, *In Praise of Slowness: How a Worldwide Movement Is Challenging the Cult of Speed*, New York: HarperCollins [2004], 4.

2 *In Praise of Slowness*, 4-5.

3 *In Praise of Slowness*, 253.

4 Franz Kafka, translator Malcom Pasley, *The Collected Aphorism*, (London: Syrens, Penguis, 1994), 27.

5 William Ernest Henley, Modern British Poetry, Louis Untermeyer, ed. New York, Harcourt, Brace and Howe, [1920], iii–xxv.

6 Orson F. Whitney, "The Soul's Captain," *Improvement Era*, May 1926, opposite inside front cover.

7 Parley P. Pratt, *Key to the Science of Theology*, Salt Lake City: Deseret Book, 1973, 101.

8 *USA Today*, Nov. 15, 2006, 10:55 PM ET , online edition.

9 Eve Conant, "Nap Quest." *Newsweek*, Feb 12, 2007, online edition.

10 *Newsweek*, online edition.

I have tried diet after diet after diet and have given up and felt like a failure. After reading the Bridell diet, however, I feel like there is hope! C.W.

———

What a diet! I have been "enlightened" in more ways than one. A.R.

———

This poetic diet has slowed down my life as well as decreasing my caloric intake. K.B.

———

Thank you for this wonderful diet, I am losing my weight slowly and so pleasantly! G.C.

———

The Bridell diet has made a profound difference in our family. Your "diet" is the most effective approach we have read; the results are gratifying and the effort has been made so much easier as we understand and appreciate the correlation between mind, body and spirit. L.M.

———

I am an avid fan. Thank you for your approach and insight; it works for me. It is the best approach I've seen so far. J.B.

———

I lost my wife two years ago after 36 years of marriage and five children. My adjustment has been difficult, and I have looked for things to keep me from gaining weight and doing other unhealthy things. Your articles have given me many good, practical ideas. J.F.

Your column has given me a different kind of hope and a renewed desire to truly lose weight for all of the right reasons. S.N.

––––––––

I must be ready to hear your counsel because the correlation between spiritual and physical is becoming more evident to me. I feel more spiritually blessed when I have the grace to restrain my physical appetites. K.M.

––––––––

As a doctor and an amateur theologian, I would like to observe that the Bridell diet has an approach that seems to be an "East meets West meets Gospel" approach to well-being. C.C.

––––––––

It has given diet a whole different meaning. M.S.

––––––––

The Lord has blessed (and cursed) me with strong appetites and emotions. He has also personally admonished me to control (or bridle) them. I know that as I am able to accomplish this task I will be able to emphasize the positive aspects of such a gift and do great things. Your diet has most certainly been an essential tool in this pursuit. J.B.

––––––––

I have faithfully read this new and revolutionary diet, trying to digest as much of it as I can. I have loved every morsel. K.L.

––––––––

I believe in the principles and have applied them successfully. It is the epitome of sage and sane advice. J.F.

I especially appreciate the fact that you are using spiritual principles and examples to help us understand our behavior, desires, motivations, etc. Not only does it help people eat better and lose weight, but, hopefully, also improve their spirituality and strength to endure. C.H.

———————

I have lost 15 pounds so far and am continuing to use [these principles] in my life. Thank you for bringing me new ways of looking at things. M.B.

———————

I have lost 12 lbs. so far. This is the first diet that's really made any sense to me, and the first I haven't had anything to rebel against!! I have enjoyed eating all of my favorite foods, but I have also learned to gauge when I am reasonably filled. This is a new feeling, but I am learning to trust it and it is working. And you were right–I am starting to crave more fruits and vegetables. It's also pretty amazing to think I have poetry inside of me. C.P.

———————

Thanks for your delightful and practical writing. It has been a long time since I have bridled a horse, but I find this new kind of bridle challenging and delightful. E.C.

———————

Great approach! I've made wonderful changes in my thinking and my eating. T.W.

———————

I have noticed that you are right about my body (when intake is limited to half) craving good food to get the nutrition it needs. I have studied nutrition for years and I know all about what not to eat, but learning what TO eat has been a challenge. This eat-half concept has really motivated me to dig into my huge healthy recipe collection and start learning how to feed myself and my family well. J.M.

I am an 80-plus widowed female, living alone. I haven't found words to express my gratitude for such enlightening information. The food diet has helped me lose 20 pounds, but even that is not so valuable as the spiritual aspect of the diet. A.H.

———

I have discovered flavors and tastes I never knew of before. Somehow I feel so much more at peace and in tune with the spirit. W.T.

———

I will be telling family and friends about your diet—anyone who wants to lose weight and, especially, anyone who feels the need for more spiritual enlighten-ment (that describes most all of us). S.D.

———

Much more reasonable and doable than all the other fad diets out there. I think your approach is the best way to achieve a PERMANENT healthy lifestyle and the best way to respect the gift of our bodies. G.D.

———

I have long believed in the true principles you teach--that our physical fitness is so closely connected to our emotional and spiritual fitness. S.R.

———

This diet has totally changed the way I think about eating. R.P.

———

The Bridell diet has had such profound effect. It helps us bridle our passions and gain more joy in physical and spiritual ways. L.N.

———

Thanks for the new perspective on life. N.R.

My weight loss now exceeds 20 pounds, and my colleagues cannot believe that my lifestyle adjustment is working. S.A

Thank you for helping me realize just what I am doing to myself. I am bound and determined to stick with this and be a better me, in all aspects of my life. I think I understand better just what our bodies can do and should be like. D.P.

Thanks so much for you insight. Please continue to minister to those with a heartbreaking addiction that is just as destructive as drugs or alcohol, but does-n't receive the same help or compassion that other addictions have. D.G.

The plan is simple. Simple to start, but not hard to keep going either. It just makes sense. J.S.

As I have read each installment, the principles espoused have all "rung" true with me. Some of the principles I had stumbled upon myself before I had read your diet, and you gave them a voice. LH

My favorite part about your approach is the linking of the physical with the spiritual and mental/emotional. I don't believe any real, long-lasting benefits can happen without addressing all three. T.C.

I do appreciate so much the spiritual aspect, because I do believe that dieting and eating issues are definitely more than just having "will power" as I hear. J.R.

Thank you for a great new approach to dieting and life. I have a long way to go but you've given me a way to go, and in "bite-sized" pieces that really work. L.S.

———————

The emotional and spiritual aspect of your series so very often had a tremendous impact on my outlook. D.F.

———————

I love the horse analogies and how they helped me really understand the body, mind, spirit differentiation analogies. S.C.

———————

The half plate idea (especially when eating out) has helped me control my portions. I try using a smaller plate at home and listening to what my body is saying. J.F.

———————

Thanks for taking the time to address the entire realm of dieting and bringing to light one of our missions here on earth–which is to learn not only to control our appetites but also to understand, care for, and master our mortal bodies. D.A.

———————

I enjoy my food more even while I eat less. The quality of the food I eat has vastly improved as well as the kind of food I WANT to eat! A.T.

———————

What worked for me: eating half portions, slowly, with a glass of water beforehand. Being thankful, savoring the food, and relating [the principles] to the spiritual self as well. The idea is great. B.E.

———————

My friends and I are starting a support group based on the principles of Bridell. K.S.

I have seen a change in my physical body, but really the best change is in my spiritual body. Thank you, thank you. I have learned so much and been so motivated by this wonderful adventure. K.B.

––––––––––

I love the new way I have of thinking about food and life. It is amazing how bridling even the passion of food helps me be more aware and contemplative of the things around me. H.C.

––––––––––

As a compulsive eater, I've found that using a 12-Step program in concert with your plan has blessed me very much. I have used your "diet" as my food plan and to define my abstinence and it has greatly blessed my life. A.P.

––––––––––

I have read a lot of diet and self-help books through the years, and yours is by far the very best. The advice is so simple yet so profound, and I love your writing style. It is very straight forward and to-the-point, not "wordy" as so many advice books are. J.R.

––––––––––

What you are saying does make a lot of sense. I especially like the way it ties the physical, mental, and spiritual together, and how the same basic principles can be applied to all three. I know in my case that when I apply correct principles to the physical and mental aspects of my being, the spiritual aspect does much better. K.J.

––––––––––

I love the way your diet works. M.M.